Myriam Ad

Sarah's Compass to Inner Peace

How to Overcome Negativity and Prevent Burnout Naturally

A self-help book

Coverdesign: Myriam Adams

Covergrafik background picture: clipdealer

Disclaimer: This book is a novel with a fictitious story and fictitious characters. All descriptions and instructions in this book are examples of a fictional story. They do not replace any medical, psychological, psychotherapeutic or other therapy or treatment. No liability is accepted for any consequences of the use of examples from the novel. The author is neither a doctor nor an alternative medicine practitioner. All self-help tips within should be discussed in advance with a doctor or therapist that you trust.

Publication and distribution are authorised by the author, who can be contacted at Myriam Adams, c/o Block Services, Stuttgarter Str. 106, 70736 Fellbach, Germany

ISBN 978-3-9827205-0-0

Dedicated to my children

From the bottom of my heart, big thank you to my friends for encouraging me to carry on

Natasha, Andrea, Rhiannon, Spike, Katrina, Richy and many more

Translation: Myriam and Natasha A. Lee

Contents

PREFACE

This book is for anyone interested in self-reflection, whether you are just beginning your journey or have already explored personal development in depth.

Throughout my life, I have been deeply curious about how to maintain health and happiness in a holistic way. Time and again, I have encountered the profound influence of our emotions and the subconscious mind. Many of the beliefs instilled in us during childhood may not serve us in adulthood; instead, they often develop into limiting patterns.

The subconscious mind operates through repetition, forming automatic responses that we may not even be aware of. As noted in an article from *Psychology Today*, '*The subconscious only knows what we feed it – so feed it healthy thoughts. And do it repeatedly; repetition is key.*' (How to Retrain the Negative Athlete Mindset, *Psychology Today*, October 2022).

Our subconscious can shape behaviours that our conscious mind has overlooked. Entire fields of study, such as psychoneuroimmunology, explore the connection between our emotions and overall well-being. Every stimulus first reaches us at a subconscious level before surfacing into conscious awareness. Over time, our beliefs can become automated, sometimes working against us rather than for us.

Because the subconscious mind communicates in images and symbols, working with visualisation techniques can be a powerful way to reconnect with your inner self.

The self-help techniques in this book have guided me through times of crisis, helping me to regain my inner balance. While this book does not aim to provide an exhaustive explanation of every method—there is already extensive literature on the subject—it serves as a guide to raise awareness of what might still be missing. Through personal insights and encouraging examples, it seeks to inspire you to continue on your path towards achieving your personal goals.

A compass offers direction; the next step is to navigate the journey.

I sincerely wish all readers holistic well-being and inner peace.

With my best wishes, Myriam Adams

Annotation:

The images in this story come either from Sarah's grandmother's book or from Sarah's own drawings. While they may not directly depict Sarah's experiences, she was often struck by how similar people's struggles could be. Looking back, she found it remarkable that, despite her grandmother having written the journal twenty years earlier, the drawings seemed to mirror her own circumstances. And, as fate would have it, she always stumbled upon the ones that resonated most—just when she needed them.

CHAPTER 1 - SARAH FEELS LONELY

'Love is stronger than anything else,' her grandmother had always said.
'All beginnings are hard,' her father had recently reminded her. Great. A move like this was pure stress, and Sarah had no idea where to start. She felt torn, trapped in a slump. Two voices echoed inside her: one urging her to embrace her grandmother's unwavering positivity, the other pulling her towards cold, hard realism.

Caught between the devil and the deep blue sea, she took the only option left—moving back into her father's flat. As she stepped inside, a wave of emptiness washed over her. Facing her new truth, she realised that the cold, abandoned room reflected her innermost self. She was petrified.

Sarah's gaze drifted into the dark abyss outside. Heavy rain pounded against the window and the porch, its relentless drumming drowning out all other sounds. Even the rain had a right to exist—she knew that. But why today of all days? She longed for sunshine to warm her and soothe her shattered heart.

Frustration gnawed at her, a hollow ache left behind after her boyfriend had abandoned her without warning—just when she needed him most. How could she ever forgive such betrayal?

She lay on her bed, staring at the ceiling, unsure how to fill the emptiness of the day. Inside, she felt as desolate as a barren desert, her tears long since dried.

Then, suddenly, she thought she heard her cat. A faint sound at first—a soft squeak—before it melted into a familiar, comforting purr.

Or was it just a trick of her imagination? Sarah couldn't be sure—the rain was still too loud, muffling every other sound.

Still, something urged her to check. She crouched down and peered under her bed—and there, staring back at her, were the familiar eyes of her favourite cat.

But wait—what was that lying in the dust beside Amruk?

She reached out, fingers brushing against the worn cover as she pulled out a small book. A black notebook with red edges and corners.

Her grandmother's journal.

How on earth had it ended up there?

CHAPTER 2 - THE DISCOVERY

Sarah shook the dust from the booklet and gave it a quick blow, sending a small cloud into the air. She sneezed, momentarily startled, before marveling at the body's remarkable ability to clear itself. The nose—a natural filter, trying to keep dirt and dust from entering.

She felt an almost magnetic pull toward the book. It was her grandmother's diary—the one filled with personal insights, the lessons she had gathered from countless workshops and seminars. Sarah remembered the day her grandmother had given it to her for her 16th birthday. Back then, she hadn't known what to make of it.

But now... could this be the answer she had been searching for?

Only last night, her friend had assured her that the universe delivers quickly—you just have to ask. And yet, how could it have known that the guidance she needed had been hiding under her bed all along?

Settling into her old bed, she reached for a handkerchief and gently wiped the neglected cover. No longer abandoned, no longer gathering dust—this journal was finally back where it belonged. As she waited for her cat to curl up beside her, she took a deep breath and opened it.

Her grandmother had handed it to her with a smile, saying, "*Do with it as you please – add your own notes and experiences. One day, you'll cherish it.*"

Now, Sarah could hardly wait to turn the first page. More than anything, she needed a new chapter in her life.

As Sarah opened the booklet, she instinctively knew this was the silver lining her soul had been yearning for – like a parched desert absorbing a single drop of water. What she didn't realise at the time was that this old notebook had the power to transform her life completely. This, without a doubt, would be the breakthrough she so desperately needed.

Inside, her grandmother had carefully inscribed her maiden name in elegant handwriting, marking it as her own. She must have treasured this book for a long time. Sarah suddenly recalled how her grandmother's initials had once been carved into the bark of the great oak tree in her parents' garden, a silent testament to the past.

The first entry was a quote from Martin Luther: *"Even if I knew that the world would end tomorrow, I would still plant an apple tree today."*

Sarah longed to find that same strength within herself. As her old world gradually crumbled, this was exactly what she needed: faith and a fresh, healthy start. It was high time to plant new ideas and let them grow.

'You can paint the world in shades of grey or light, see it through sorrow or bathe it in bright,' her granddad had repeated over and over. Now, for the first time, Sarah was truly trying to understand these words —not just with her mind, but with her heart.

Lost in her melancholic thoughts, Sarah's mind wandered aimlessly. Without thinking, she flipped open a page of the journal.

'Visualising a metaphor can heal anything. Just add a little spiritual ecstasy. '

Yes, enthusiasm and bliss—that was exactly what she needed.

'The magical world within is your inner healer.'

Next to this powerful phrase were hurriedly written words: 'But first, you must transform your mentality of being a victim. Become aware of old belief systems and past conditioning.

Identify the flaw in the system, or you risk running a counter-program that can undermine your visualisation.'

Sarah took a deep breath. *'Well, when I visualise and imagine something, it can only reach its full potential if I don't have a counter-program running,'* she thought. A counter-programme that told her, for example, that she wasn't worthy. Another deep breath. Her grandma's words echoed in her mind, a soothing reminder of the universe's power: *'When your mind feels empty, my darling, and everything seems to be falling apart, take a deep breath and trust the universe. Or ask God for help. The God who resides in your heart. He is always there for you.'* Her grandma believed that the terms God, universe, and divine energy were interchangeable.

'Follow your intuition. What kind of world would we live in without the grace of charity? Many of the prayers and allegories in the Bible offer valuable guidance. Take Mark 11:24, for example: *'Therefore I say unto you, whatsoever things ye desire, when ye pray, believe that ye have received them, and ye shall have them.'* There is much truth in that. Today, you might say, find the vibrational match to what you want to manifest. Doesn't that mean the same thing?'.

Since childhood, Sarah had admired Mary and was in awe of Jesus' unconditional love. Both Mary and Jesus had remained central to her prayers. As she reflected, goosebumps spread across her arms, and an inner knowing washed over her intuitively – she was on the right path.

Sarah read in her grandma's diary: 'The power of imagination is immense. Think of biting into a lemon. Visualise it long enough, and soon you'll feel saliva gathering in your mouth. Close your eyes and picture yourself slicing a juicy lemon into pieces. Now, cut one slice in half. Lemon juice drips onto your fingers, and you lick them. Oh, it's so sour. Are you there yet? Is your mouth already watering? Yes? And where's the lemon? It's not on the kitchen table. It only existed in your mind. And yet, just by thinking about it, you've created a physical reaction. Now, can you channel this power of positive imagination into other areas of your life?'

Sarah had made the decision to move into her own flat. She couldn't stay with her dad forever, feeling like the odd one out. At times, she felt like a piggy in the middle, constantly trying to please everyone around her. Lost and uncertain about her purpose, she often felt like she was being pushed around by the people in her life.

Her dad had a new partner who wasn't exactly welcoming of extra family members, and once again, Sarah found herself feeling unwanted and redundant. It was a feeling she knew all too well, one that stung deeply, and it saddened her to realise that this sense of rejection had become almost second nature.

Thoughts form inner images.
Inner images serve the power of imagination
The power of imagination can move mountains!

A few days later, however, the tide turned. Sarah had a stroke of luck. A colleague was moving in with her boyfriend, and her old flat became available. It was a small, cosy two-bedroom flat just around the corner. Sarah was over the moon and quickly accepted the offer.

'Gosh, you're in luck!' her friend exclaimed, sharing in her excitement. But despite her friend's enthusiasm, Sarah couldn't shake the feeling that her luck was too good to be true. Why not? Other people seemed to stumble upon good fortune without much effort. Yet Sarah felt like she had to work tirelessly for everything, as if happiness or luck was something she didn't deserve.

To her, life often felt more like dodging bullets than picking daisies. So, when she considered the situation with the flat, a part of her wondered if she truly deserved it. Why did she feel this way sometimes?

CHAPTER 3 - FIRST INSIGHTS

By evaluating your thoughts, you direct energy towards a particular thing or situation. If that's not something you want, simply shift your focus to the situation you'd prefer to create instead. In doing so, you redirect your energy. There's an old saying: **Energy flows where attention goes**. In Western society, many people only believe in what they can see, dismissing spiritual experiences as a waste of time, reserved only for daydreamers who are "away with the fairies." Reading this, Sarah decided to believe that there was more to life than what the naked eye could perceive.

OK - what is uplifting for me?
What do I need right now?

Sometimes, Sarah felt as though she was missing something. Was she able to transform these feelings? The nagging sense that she wasn't worthy of happiness. Could this be something she had inherited? She often heard stories about her unlucky aunt, the black sheep of the family. Had Sarah subconsciously taken on some of her aunt's traits? Was it possible she had inherited this sense of inadequacy, this hidden guilt from her family? Could that even happen? Or perhaps she had created this feeling of lack herself. Why did she feel unworthy of love? And didn't her boyfriend's treatment of her mirror that very feeling? As if, deep down, she wasn't trusted with important matters, as though she were to be treated like a child. It seemed that everything she took on herself was doomed to fail from the start.

This profound insight was far from flattering, but at the same time, Sarah felt a sense of relief. By taking back responsibility, she realised she had the power to rewrite her old limiting beliefs and transform them into something positive. It was certainly worth a try!

Though this realisation wasn't exactly thrilling, it brought with it a sense of liberation. Sarah understood that she could reshape her old beliefs, reorganising them in a way that would serve her better. It was worth a shot.

As her old world crumbled, Sarah clung to the journal, searching for a new sense of meaning in her life.

Master your mind!

Whatever you believe about yourself will shape your reality!

Let your resiliance and compassion shine!

From a turbulent mind – to radiant sunshine in your heart. 😊

You can read Sarah's thoughts in *italic.*

(The pictures are from the journal.)

How to boost your morale:

Think back to a time when you felt completely defeated—when you thought, *This is it. Game over.* Maybe you were certain you'd lose your job, your home, or something else important to you. But then, a few days later, things weren't as bad as they seemed. Perhaps the outcome wasn't what you initially expected, or maybe it was, and you felt like your life was falling apart. Yet, here you are—still standing, still moving forward.

More often than not, our worst fears don't play out as catastrophically as we imagine. And even when life takes an unexpected turn, we adapt, we push through, and we grow stronger. Every challenge you've overcome has built resilience and endurance within you.

So keep going. Persevere. You never know what opportunity might be waiting just around the corner.

Sometimes, it's just your inner monkey mind dragging you from pillar to post. If we can learn to quieten this restless chatter, life could be so much more peaceful. (*Of course, we're talking about unnecessary psychological anxiety here – if you're about to be robbed, then by all means, run for your life!*)

Sarah could think of countless examples where her fears had run wild, only for everything to turn out just fine in the end. No real drama, just her mind playing tricks on her.

But what's worse—the reality of a situation, or the way you perceive and judge it in your mind?

She was tired of the endless cycle of negative thoughts and self-doubt.

Determined to break free from this pattern, Sarah knew it was time for a new approach to life. The change started now.

Eureka! Not what happened,
but my inner evaluation of it
is what is crucial.
Because not everyone gets sick after being
shouted at. - When do I feel insulted?
I need a pick-me-up ü

Give your immune system a push up:

What is your anxiety about? Has it already happened? *Yes, my boyfriend has abondoned me*

Trust your intuition. *What intuition?*

Energy flows where attention goes.

Stay true to your own feelings.

What truly resonates with me?

Yes, the law of resonance. What was that about again?

Maybe I should try to turn it around. *Instead of feeling anxious about taking responsibility, I could embrace the challenge. Instead of worrying about not being able to pay the rent, I could trust that a solution will always present itself. Instead of fearing being alone when I'm sick, I could have faith that someone will be there to care for me. Maybe I should turn these feelings around:*

I am grateful!

Grateful for this new flat that became available.

Grateful that my colleague chose me to 'inherit' it.

Grateful that I can afford to make it my home.

Feel the Love

Sarah took her time. After a few deep breaths, a wave of gratitude gently washed over her. She had also considered a plan B – if everything else failed, she could always return to her dad's or move in with her aunt.

As Einstein famously said, **'The most important question you can ask yourself is this: Is the universe a friendly place?'**

Sarah paused. No, the universe wasn't a friendly place.

'Her boyfriend went AWOL with her best friend, and she felt completely betrayed by both of them.
To hell with Einstein – what did he know?'

'Okay, first things first – take a deep breath. Focus on your breathing,' she reminded herself. Just last week, she had told her colleague the same thing: emotional first aid – stabilize yourself with your breath! And yes, it really works.

The book stated: Ask yourself, have you truly embraced the fullness of life? Do you welcome the abundance it offers, or do you feel as though something is missing? Are you living in scarcity, or are you living in abundance? *I'm in scarcity. My boyfriend has left me.*

Do you have everything you need within you, in the essence of who you are? *Yes*

What can you do right now for yourself to feel good?

I can hate him.

Lost in thought, Sarah stared out the window.

Her chest felt heavy and burdened.

No...that's not it.

Give it another try, she thought.

What can you do for yourself now to feel better?

I'll watch some telly, make myself a nice cuppa, and grab a hot water bottle.

Minutes later, Sarah stretched out under her duvet, settling into a comfortable position. Her eyes grew heavier with each passing moment, the steady rhythm of the raindrops tapping against her window lulling her into a sense of calm.

Just before drifting off to sleep, she paused to acknowledge the things she had accomplished over the past few days. It felt different from the all-too-familiar weight of self-criticism, and as she reflected on her achievements, a sense of peace washed over her. She smiled softly and, with a lighter heart, surrendered to sleep.

Which identity do I choose?

Who will I be?

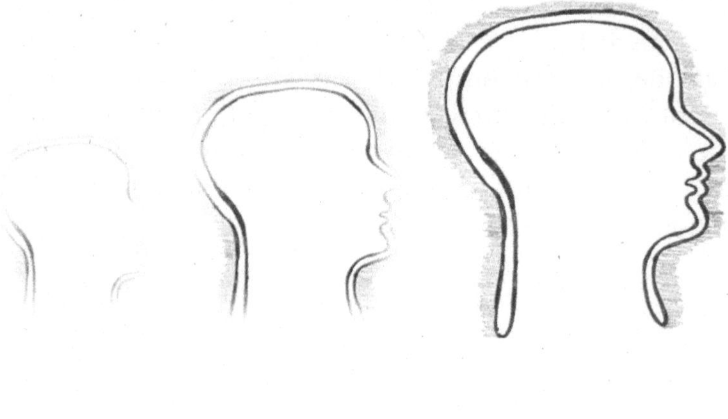

Let an idea in your mind become reality

CHAPTER 4 - TURNING TABLES

The next day, Sarah felt ready to take on the world. 'One step at a time,' she told herself. 'I advised my colleague to take good care of herself and trust her intuition. Well, honestly, I can do the same! I deserve as much love as anyone else.'

She decided to work through her granny's list, one step at a time.

Wholeheartedly she started with her list:

Turning Around Negativity:

1. **Instead of**: I hate him, he still owes me.

New Mantras:

- *I can manage on my own. Time to get going.*
- *I'm on the path of healing.*

2. **Instead of:** I will repeat my mother's mistakes in order to feel closer to her on a subconscious level.

- *I replace the bond with my mother with positivity. We don't have to repeat our parents' mistakes.*

  Explanation:
  Instead of being fixated on trouble and attracting relationships that mirror my inner turmoil, I will remind myself that I am love. There is no need to repeat my mum's patterns when choosing partners. Mum often fell for the same type of man—hook, line, and sinker—and they were never suitable partners. Perhaps my subconscious clung to this negative pattern, believing it would bring me closer to her. By replacing this inherited behaviour with a positive trait of my mum's, I can release this old, limiting pattern.

- *I will replace the bond with my mother by embracing her love for animals, particularly dogs.*

3. **Instead of**: I am a failure, betrayed and sold out.

- Where does my focus lie? Do I focus on my deficits, or do I choose to concentrate on the power within me? Everything I want: Love, recognition and affection, I first give to myself. I will satisfy my needs with love and affection. I will be like a magnet which attracts what I already hold within. I vibrationally match the good things in life. So everything I am within, will eventually be reflected on the outside. I am a vibrational match to the good things in life. I will operate from this level of energy: Love overflow. *Yes*!

4. Why am I able to calm myself down?

- Because I've successfully calmed myself before. *Because I believe in myself, and I trust my ability to find peace.*
- Everything I desire – love, affection, and approval – I will first give to myself. *Ooooohhhhh, great! I've just figured that out myself! Yeah!*
- How do I value the simple things in life? How can I create a healthy work-life balance? *I'll take a break, make myself a cuppa, and enjoy it wholeheartedly.*
  How can I calm my thoughts and find peace within? *By focusing on what I truly want, I'll get my priorities straight. Right now, it's about packing boxes for the move – letting go of everything I no longer need and releasing material things that have become a burden.*

- How do I manage to focus on what is important to me right now? *I'll take a deep breath, pause to think, and take one step at a time.*

- Make a list of everything that occupies my mind. Once I tick it off, it's done. *Exactly.*

- I stay balanced and avoid getting sidetracked. To make this even more effective, I'll reframe it positively: I am focusing on my desired outcome: serenity and vitality.

  Yes, vitality. I can do this! I will pack up the boxes for the move. If I feel overwhelmed, I can ask for help – maybe someone can assist me in carrying them to the car.

- I am allowing myself to be happy! *Mmm, my mum used to say she had a counterprogram to happiness. Do I have that too? Do I allow myself to be happy? No. Why not?*

- Adopt an identity you wish to embody:
  I am ______________

  I am happy in my new flat.

- *I am a successful blogger. And so on.*

- Use the '4711' breathing technique. *What is this? I'll ask duckduckgo.*

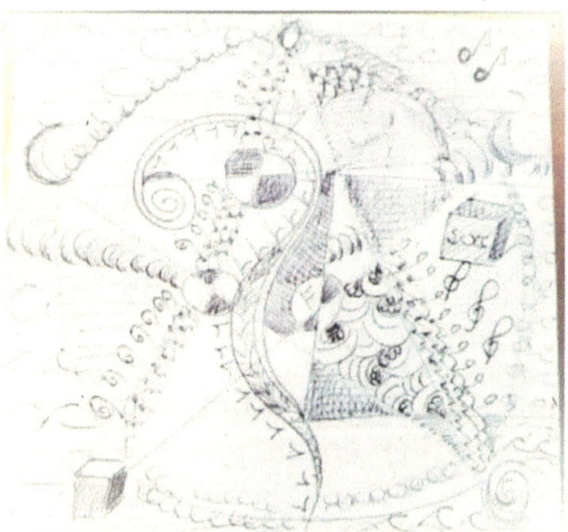

The day had gone exceptionally well, and Sarah had packed a mountain of moving boxes. Humming and buzzing with energy, she felt carefree and on top of the world. She made a mental note to call her friend Jo as soon as the move was done. Jo was the best foot massage therapist she knew, and she had taught Sarah the art of reflexology. Ever since, they'd taken turns massaging each other's feet. It had become a beautiful ritual—a much-needed relief for body, mind, and soul.

Sometimes, Sarah forgot just how simple it was to create moments of joy. The last massage had been pure magic. Endorphins surged through her body, and for a brief moment, her mind went quiet. Her soul seemed to float freely, drifting through time and space, while her body naturally found its balance again.

All the good reasons
for your feelings

Imbalance manifests itself in discomfort

Inner peace can be created
by working through old negative beliefs

Feeling exhausted, Sarah drifted into a restless sleep. Abruptly, she woke in the middle of the night, her thoughts once again consumed by her absent mother.

There was a gaping hole inside her — a vast chasm that seemed to widen whenever someone casually remarked, 'Your mother abandoned you!' Sarah felt trapped in an endless cycle of pain, unable to heal the wounds that stemmed from her mother's absence and the sense of rejection. It was like a wound that constantly reopened, never allowing her to recover.

Her mother was still alive, still kicking, but Sarah couldn't understand why she hadn't cared for her when she needed her the most. Why hadn't she made more of an effort than sending a Christmas postcard? The occasional phone call was barely a gesture. For Sarah, the loss of her mother felt like the loss of her very life.

If her mother had died, at least there would have been closure. She could have grieved, truly grieved. But instead, Sarah was left suspended in this state of limbo. Her mother wasn't dead. She hadn't died in a tragic accident. She hadn't even been in an accident. No, Sarah was grieving for a different kind of loss — the loss of a childhood that could never be reclaimed, the loss of a mother who had chosen a life without her. When her mother had decided to emigrate to Thailand, she had made the painful decision to leave Sarah behind, as if she had no place in her new life.

'God child, you wouldn't have wanted her to take you with her anyway!' her aunt moaned, her words hitting Sarah like a cold wave. Sarah longed for her aunt to give her the space to just *be* herself. She was desperate for answers, for a chance to untangle the mess of emotions that had been festering inside her. But instead, everyone around her jumped to conclusions, feeding her their opinions and half-baked speculations. She had never been given the opportunity to process her own feelings about her mother abandoning her. Everything had always been suppressed and locked away.

She wasn't supposed to talk about her mother. "*Don't you dare think about your mother! Don't even mention emotions!*" She'd been warned time and again. It was as though acknowledging her pain could pull her into a deep, chaotic abyss. Emotions, it seemed, were dangerous territory.

In a flash, Sarah understood why she had chosen her boyfriend in the first place. Why he had seemed so appealing. He told her what to do, how to think, and mapped out every aspect of her day. He made the decisions. Looking at it now, he was the perfect substitute for a parent. She had subconsciously chosen a partner who reflected the absence she felt in her relationship with her own parents.

This relationship was far from balanced. He had the money. He pulled the strings. He dictated the terms, ensuring she stayed in line. Deep down, Sarah knew that her boyfriend had inadvertently stepped into the role of a parent—her parent. And that realization stung.

Suddenly, Sarah understood why this move was so important: it was her chance to find herself. To finally feel her own emotions, free from the weight of someone else's emotional world. She was tired of being told what was supposedly going on deep inside her. No, it was time for a journey of self-discovery—to figure out what she truly liked and disliked, without anyone else's influence.

It was time to stand on her own two feet—no boyfriend, no father, no aunt. And certainly not her mother. This was her moment to uncover her own desires, to face both her strengths and her flaws. It carried a taste of freedom. The sense of empowerment was exhilarating!

She was ready to grow up, to make her own decisions, and to embrace adulthood. "Make your own mistakes," she had heard that advice a thousand times. And now, it rang clear in her mind. "Don't be afraid of taking the wrong turn or making mistakes. Wrong decisions are still better than no decisions at all. Stagnation is like a slow death. Stay in the flow. Follow your dreams. Embrace mistakes as experiences, because they are exactly that. Once you've made a mistake, you'll know which path to choose—and which one to avoid.

She sat down on her bed, her eyes drifting to the diary. Flipping to the next page, she began to read:

'Imagine you're walking into a party. The moment you step through the door, you instinctively pick up on the atmosphere—whether it feels warm and inviting or tense and uncomfortable. You don't need anyone to tell you; you can sense the energy in the room. Now, let's turn that around. Aren't we all energy beings? And if we can sense the energy of a room, can't others sense what we carry within us?

What happens if we hold onto old feelings of shame or guilt? If, deep down, we believe we don't deserve to take up space? What if, without even realizing it, we keep ourselves small as a form of self-punishment? Could it be that others subconsciously pick up on this, treating us accordingly—perhaps dismissing us, overlooking us, or even treating us unkindly?

Have you ever noticed how people seem to sense when you're having a bad day? That's why it's important to acknowledge these patterns and recognize the reasons behind them. Even if being overlooked has felt painful, what if there was a good reason for it? What if, by shifting your inner perspective, you could transform your energy—and in turn, change the way the world responds to you?'

Intuition where are you?

Exhausted, she shuffled into the bathroom and glanced at her reflection in the mirror. A zombie stared back at her, confirming what she already knew—she was long overdue for sleep.

It took a while for her mind to settle. Sleep was like a temporary surrender of the ego, a small death of consciousness, leaving her entirely at the mercy of her subconscious. Through dreams, it whispered its messages, trying to be heard.

An intriguing thought struck her—what was her subconscious trying to tell her? Maybe it was time to start writing down her dreams.

The next morning, Sarah made a fresh list:

- **A loving hug to myself.**
- **Main goal:** Moving into my new flat!
- Set a deadline for the move and arrange help.
- Have *all* moving boxes packed and ready in time.
- *A rolling stone gathers no moss*—no dwelling on the past, just keep moving forward!

- **My rewards:**
    - Enjoying well-deserved breaks with delicious food and soul-soothing music.
    - Brewing a comforting cup of tea.
    - Listening to my favorite songs.
    - Stroking one of my cats.
    - Sitting in the sun for 15 minutes, feeling the warmth on my skin.

From theory into practice: **a loving hug to myself!**

Sarah closed her eyes and recalled a beautiful moment with her friend. For once, she allowed herself to truly *savor* the feeling—something she had never done before. 'It's amazing how the power of imagination can work.'

Sarah set herself a **14-day deadline** – clear goals, sharp focus! In hindsight, it was a brilliant move. Her subconscious seemed to align with the deadline, fueling her with the drive she needed to get things done. No more excuses!

The diary made Sarah feel deeply connected to her beloved grandmother, and that warmth filled her heart. She reminisced about cozy afternoons at her grandmother's house, knowing she would always hold a special place in her heart. This mutual love had created an unbreakable bond, one that still offered her strength. It was time to focus on these uplifting moments – to be mindful of what nourished her soul rather than dwelling on what drained her. With gratitude, Sarah cherished the love and wisdom her grandmother had given her.

Her thoughts drifted back to her ex-boyfriend. How could she set healthy boundaries without letting resentment consume her? Seeking clarity, she called her grandmother, grateful for her simple yet profound wisdom.

'Sarah, you've probably heard that the world we live in is one of duality. There is day and night, light and dark, hot and cold—apparent opposites. That's why it's called duality (from the Latin *dualitas* = duality). But have you ever wondered where our soul comes from? Does it originate from this world of contrasts? Everyone must find their own answer to that question. Some believe the soul exists beyond this material world, untouched by duality. And if that's true, then love can flow freely on a soul level—beyond conflict, beyond opposition.

You can love every human being on this deeper level,' her grandmother continued. 'But in the world of duality, it's essential to set healthy boundaries—so that your own needs are honored too. Sometimes, the other person simply isn't capable of functioning in a balanced way. That's why it's about finding an equilibrium between giving and receiving, rooted in mutual respect.

Right now, the most important thing you can do is establish those boundaries, in whatever form feels right for you. Your intuition—your subconscious—will guide you toward the approach that best serves both you and those involved. If you can, be an example of wholeness and connection. Show what it means to stand in your own strength while remaining open to love.

Every situation is unique, and each one calls for its own solution,' her grandmother continued. 'Hate isn't the opposite of love—it's the absence of it. A separation from love. A disconnection from our true source. Maybe, in some cases, it's even a cry for help.

You have the power to forgive and release on a soul level, to love unconditionally. But in this world of duality, you must also set healthy boundaries. Go within and ask yourself: Does this feel true for me? Find your own truth. Trust your feelings. Have faith in your own wisdom—I know you'll find the right path forward.'

> 'What is worse? What really happened?
> Or your inner judgement about it?'

The last sentence felt like a warm embrace. Her grandmother believed in her. That trust enveloped her like a comforting blanket, providing solace and reassurance. She stroked her favorite cat, feeling its soft fur beneath her fingers. A shiver of joy ran down her spine. For a fleeting moment, she had a vision—just a glimpse—but it felt good. It felt real.

'Come on, baby! You got this!' she chirped to herself, a newfound determination rising within her.

'Wait, I have to tell you something!' her grandma laughed. 'I accidentally had a shower in bed yesterday! Grandad and I were laughing our heads off. I just stretched out my arms, and somehow, I must have turned on the old water tap with my elbow! Can you believe it? Our bed is right underneath the old tap from where the sink used to be. We removed the sink, but not the tap yet. My mattress was soaking! We had to sleep in the guest room.'

Sarah burst into laughter, picturing the scene. She loved how her grandma could laugh at her own mishaps. No one is perfect—and honestly, who cares? As long as you are downright lovable, that's all that really matters.

😉

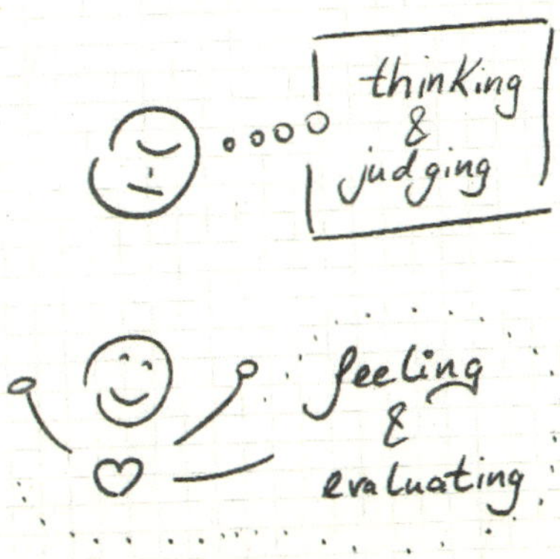

Mucking out!

Sarah felt a surge of elation. After snapping a few photos of her favourite handbag, she tossed them aside. Who needed so many bags or mugs, anyway?

Full of vigour, she made a decision right then and there to clear out her emotional baggage too.

Emotional Freedom

The journal held more treasures inside:

What old beliefs am I still clinging to? Or rather, which old beliefs does my subconscious continue to hold on to or follow? Do they still serve me? What exactly is my subconscious? It governs all the processes I don't consciously influence—like breathing and digestion. The subconscious mind can develop automatic patterns that we're not always aware of. Our feelings, thoughts, and actions are also shaped by the subconscious. It controls behaviours that might be neglected by the conscious mind.

There are specialised fields, such as psychoneuroimmunology, that explore the connections between our emotions and our body. Every stimulus first reaches us at the subconscious level before making its way to the conscious mind. Beliefs can become ingrained in the subconscious and, at times, work against us. Since the subconscious communicates through images, using visualisations, images, and symbols is an effective way to connect with your deepest self.

This enables you to bypass the critical mind and access the subconscious.

If I hold on to old behavioural patterns, they can become ingrained in my subconscious. Am I **truly self-determined** and sovereign, or am I being influenced by others?

Have I agreed to things in the past just to avoid arguments with my boyfriend? Is there a way to find solutions that work for both sides? How do families with multiple children navigate differing needs? What if each child wants to do something different? Are there ways to find a solution that benefits everyone?

Perhaps the key lies in understanding what each person truly wants. Maybe a shared space can be created where all needs are met, or time can be divided so that each child receives individual attention.

'Wow, this is like mental kung fu!' Sarah thought. 'New synapses are forming – work in progress!' Her mind drifted to old stories, realising that things could be much simpler than she once believed. Well, hope persists against all odds. Nothing ventured, nothing gained.

It's a shift in perception. By changing my beliefs, I can co-create the world around me. But is that really true? Only I can answer that for myself. Even if I can't manifest all my desires, I find myself more in the flow than before.

Am I separate from my divine, primordial essence? Or am I a part of it, carrying its power with me into this world of duality? Is it truly the fault of others if I struggle or feel unhappy? Am I projecting blame onto them?

What gives me greater freedom – taking responsibility for my life or relying on the unpredictable actions of others? What do I resonate with? What energy am I aligned with? Do I accept what happens around me, or am I caught in inner resistance?

In a world of separation, egos clash and attack each other. But beneath every argument, there may be a silent cry for love.

Today, I choose a new path. I surrender to the present moment.
I choose to forgive you, and I choose to forgive myself. I choose love.
I place my trust in life. I call upon the primordial source — the unmanifested force that gifted my soul this body — to free me from any guilt I may have carried or caused.
I ask the universe, this benevolent energy, to remind me always that love is the greatest power of all.
Help me create a space where we can live and love together. In this spirit, we are connected. In this space, harmony can unfold.

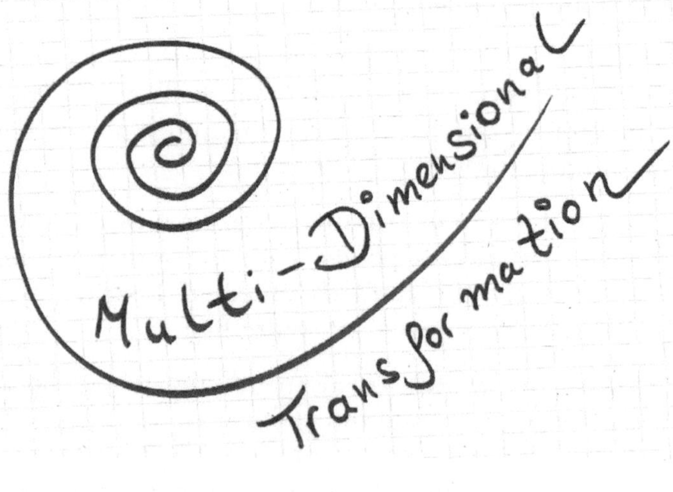

What happens when I am in resistance?

Sarah read these words in the journal and was instantly reminded of an old situation. The memory surfaced vividly:

I didn't want to go to that birthday party.

His mum's birthday. Though her actual birthday was in winter, she had a habit of celebrating in the summer. She preferred an elegant outdoor gathering—besides, she didn't want a hundred guests trampling over her living room carpet with their muddy winter shoes.

Sarah struggled with all the hoity-toity behaviour and wanted nothing to do with it. But in the end, she went—just to please her boyfriend. Looking back, maybe she should have stayed home in the first place. Turning up in a bad mood, radiating negativity, hadn't done anyone any favours.

What if she had taken a moment to reflect on her attitude before going? Could she have found a middle ground between her own feelings and her mother-in-law's wishes? Or what if she had simply chosen not to go at all?

How could she stay true to herself while also respecting the wishes of her boyfriend and mother-in-law? Was it even necessary in this particular situation? What values was she actually trying to defend? After all, it wasn't her birthday.

Maybe she could have honoured her own feelings while still attending the party—showing up as her authentic self but with kindness. Looking back, everything seemed different now. It didn't really matter as much as she had thought at the time.

In the grand scheme of things, it was just one day out of 365.

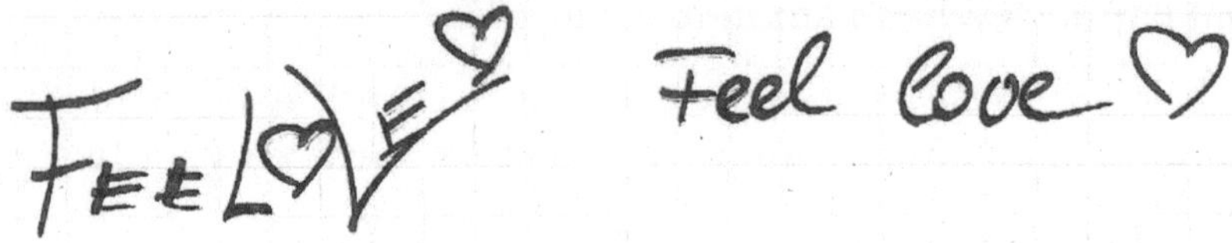

Sarah continued reading the journal: When I'm in resistance, I step out of the flow. I become disconnected from my intuition—**the very bridge to my original source**. It's like losing the connection to my inner switchboard, the point of communication with something greater.

My truth isn't found outside of me; it lies deep within. But to reach it, I must be willing to face my fears.

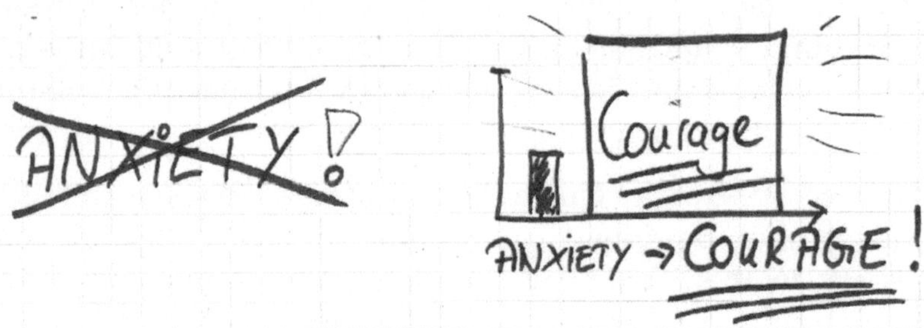

Where attention goes, energy flows. If my focus is on resistance, I may invite more resistance into other areas of my life. I could end up reinforcing the very things I don't want.

'**What you resist, persists**.' Was that from Carl Gustav Jung, or perhaps ancient Indian wisdom? Regardless of its origin, the truth resonates: when you resist something, you give it power.

So, wouldn't it be wiser to shift the focus? Focus on what you want, rather than dwelling on what might go wrong.

Nevertheless, it's also important to acknowledge the things our mind tries to avoid. Carl Gustav Jung developed what we now know as *shadow work*. Jung referred to repressed personality traits as the "shadow" aspects of the self. These traits are often tied to repression and fear. What is buried deep in the subconscious has a way of resurfacing into our conscious awareness.

There are valid reasons why these parts of ourselves are initially hidden. However, if they remain suppressed, they can drain our energy. **By integrating or becoming aware of the shadow, we open the door to transformation and growth**.

So, what exactly lies buried deep within my subconscious? What does my ego try to suppress?

Sarah recalled a nightmare she had a few nights ago. The dream mirrored her deepest fears, and she had the distinct feeling that it was time to face them rather than run from her own shadow.

"*Go through it, don't suppress it,*" her grandmother's journal advised.

Wow, there was a lot to process.

Determined to begin, Sarah grabbed a pen and started writing.

Anything to wash away the blues.

I'm afraid of:

Being rejected.

Not being loved.

In the past, rejection could have meant death. As babies or small children, we were utterly dependent on our parents, or the elders in our community, to care for us. We relied on the tribe, on the bond of the group.

No wonder my mind makes such a big deal out of it when it thinks, *"I'm not loved."* In ancient times, that would have meant certain death.

Fear of....

...is there anything else I'm afraid of?

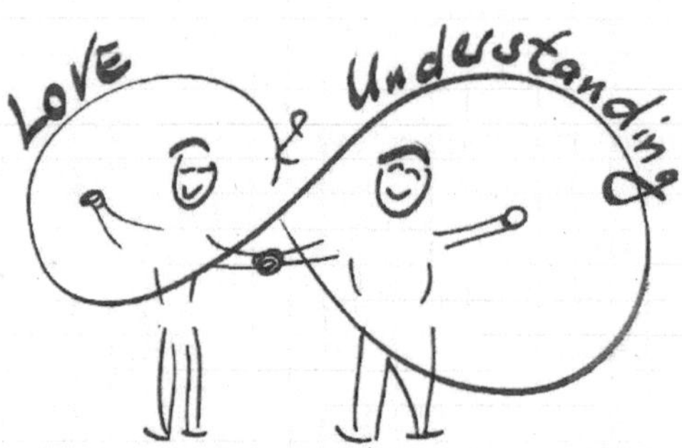

Sarah flipped through the journal and there it was, in bold letters: *Do you believe that you, or all beings, have a soul?*

'Yes! I have a soul,' she answered aloud.

But what came first—the soul or the body? She pondered the question.

If the soul came first, then there must be a Universal Law or a greater force that gave her soul a body. It meant that spirit must be above matter, she concluded.

There must be a primordial source stronger than duality, she thought.

Wow. She had to let that sink in.

That also meant that the answers to all her anxieties were deep within herself. The answers to her questions were as unique as people themselves.

How many times had she felt judged by others? There were plenty of examples. Could she flip the narrative? How did she judge herself? How did she label herself? Perhaps this was the message the universe was trying to send her. What she encountered on the outside was a reflection of what she carried within.

Maybe it was time to raise her self-worth. Time to become more self-aware and boost her self-esteem. If she could do that, it wouldn't matter so much if others judged her. In fact, they might even be kinder in their judgments—or perhaps they wouldn't judge at all.

If she felt uprooted, it was because her parents hadn't provided her with the sense of support she needed – the feeling that she would always be backed, no matter what. Lacking security, Sarah had subconsciously sought it from her parents or even substitutes, like her boyfriend.

Deep down, she expected that, at some point, they would give her the roots and the stable home she longed for. After all, she believed that was their role. But somewhere along the way, Sarah had grown up. She had survived the dramas and the valleys of tears. She had matured, but in doing so, she had also bottled up certain needs. The question now was, how much longer would she expect others to provide everything for her?

Could Sarah find that sense of integrity and stability within herself? What did she need to do? Reprogramme her subconscious? Simply endure a situation before passing judgment on it? **Instead of falling apart, she resolved to endure challenging situations.** Sarah paused for a moment, and then a powerful image came to her mind. She envisioned a great, ancient tree—its roots deep in the earth. Just as this tree could withstand the fiercest storms, she too could rise above difficult circumstances. She would give herself emotional roots. She would nurture herself, ensuring she felt more grounded, just like a tree, connecting heaven and earth.

Follow your dreams ♡

ACHIEVE your dreams!

Make a List of Old Beliefs

When you tell yourself something long enough, or when it's repeatedly told to you, a negative belief can take root. Over time, this belief becomes internalized—sometimes even subconsciously.

For instance, if you believe that not achieving a school certificate will lead to failure, your subconscious may take that as a directive and start aligning your thoughts and actions with that belief. Perhaps it's not a dramatic failure, but you might find yourself falling short of your potential. According to the law of resonance, you attract what you send out. Just like a captain steers a ship, your subconscious follows the course set by your beliefs.

Is this true? Sarah thought. She decided to test it out in a positive way and see if she could use this principle to achieve something she truly wanted.

'Put a sock in it and rephrase old negative beliefs,' her grandma cheerfully said over the phone. 'People call that belief systems.'

Sarah smiled, feeling the warmth of her grandmother's wisdom. She made herself a cup of tea, settled into her chair, and grabbed pen and paper. Within moments, she was jotting down her old beliefs, ready to transform them.

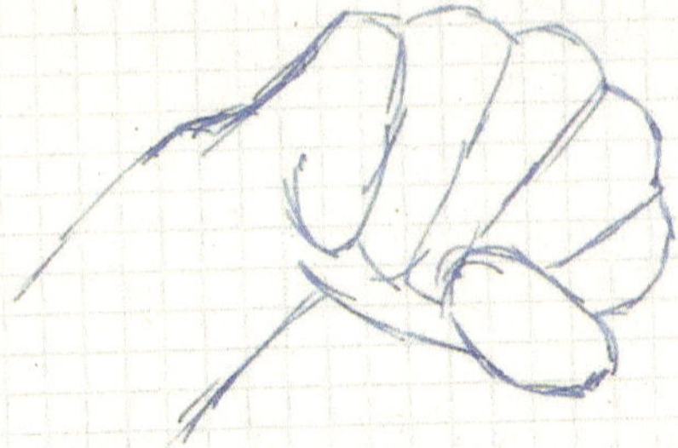

break through old beliefs!

<u>Sarahs' Old Negative Beliefs:</u>

<u>Attacking the Problem at the Root Level:</u>

1. *I'm only complete with a partner.*
2. *Without A-levels, I'll end up in the gutter.*
3. *I will never have enough time.*
4. *Only old-fashioned women cook. I'm better than that, and I don't belong in the kitchen.*
5. *If I am overweight, I am unattractive and ugly.*
6. *If I don't earn enough money, I'm a failure.*
7. *My hands are tied.*

I forgive myself...

... for decisions I made in the past.

These old beliefs really had a way of bringing her down. But Sarah quickly adapted, making a habit of replacing them with a new, positive direction. She formulated her new beliefs in such a way that they became a mantra. Small rituals helped reinforce her new mindset. It was no more time-consuming than feeding her cats every day. Now, she was feeding her hungry spirit! This new realisation ignited a spark within her, a fire that lit up her soul. Sarah's face radiated with joy!

The ritual could be as simple as chanting her positive affirmations while gazing into a candle's warm glow. She even began to create new rituals as she went along. Why not? After all, creativity is a powerful healer.

New Insights!

This was her ground zero! A clean slate, a fresh start. It was time to shed the old, embrace the new, and build something stronger from the ground up

1. I am whole – I am love.
2. I am creative and successful.
3. I operate from a place of high energy.
4. I create nourishing, delicious and healthy meals.
5. I have a beautyful body, full of rhythm and captivating charisma.
6. I am in the flow of bliss and abundance.
7. I generate this emotion to embody this vibration.

new mantra:
I am ...
I am ... (fill in)
I am a good cook
I am successful
I am homeowner
I am happy
I am love :)
use this mantra shortly after waking up
say it out loud & be happy
and / or in the evenings shortly before
falling asleep

Sarah felt so full of vigour that she accomplished more the next day than she had in days before. Wonderful! It had truly paid off to take stock and reorganise everything. Instead of being a victim of external circumstances, she had grown stronger through her experiences. Now, she knew her inner worth!

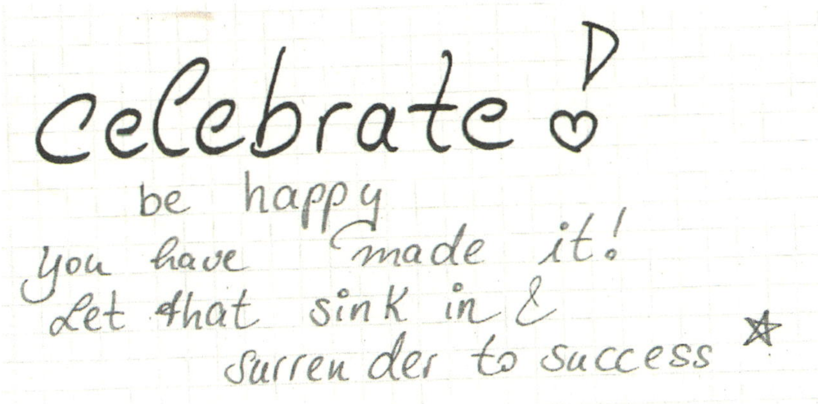

For the first time in ages she felt complete. No longer was she the defeated loser. She had rescued herself from the depths of her melancholy. Now, she was like a **phoenix, reborn from the ashes**. She was the one who embraced her divine inheritance, awakening all the divine qualities she had always carried within her. Sarah realised that this was not something new - it was her true being, her soul essence.

Or rather: she remembered it!

And that could no longer be shaken off by anyone or anything that happened on the outside!
"Never forget that!" she said to herself.

CHAPTER 9 - UNDERSTANDING SETBACKS

A couple of days later Sarah felt like she was back to square one.

Everything she tackled seemed to fail. Her father had originally planned to join her when they exchanged the keys to the flat, but his car had broken down. What now? Her stomach was on strike again, and a wave of unease washed over her. Should she call the landlord and postpone the appointment again? Or would that make her dependent on the landlord's fickleness once more? After all, he had let her down before. It was an emotional rollercoaster, and the constant ups and downs were throwing her off balance.

The more stressed she became, the more disconnected she felt from her intuition. Desperately, she needed some peace and quiet to figure out which path was the right one. It was a funny thought—*finding a solution from the inside out*. She briefly considered her options, but her focus was as stubborn as a mule heading in the wrong direction. She needed to step away from the overactive mind for a moment and approach the situation holistically. The mind was too fixated on the problem, and that only created more stress: a broken car, a cancelled appointment, no keys received. The moving date was cancelled, friends were upset because they'd already taken time off to help her. The carousel of negative thinking was spinning out of control. She decided to find her cats and made herself a calming cup of tea. Maybe, just maybe, a little pause was exactly what she needed.

over-
thinking
access
denied

If we are over-thinking,
access to our gut-feeling,
to our intuition
can be blocked.

Sarah played a game of online chess to distract herself from the mounting pressure. Suddenly, as if a switch had flipped, an insight washed over her.

She knew what she had to do. She would call her friend. And if her friend didn't have time, she would go to the meeting on her own.

In that moment, Sarah made a decision. She wouldn't wait another single day for the key to her new flat. She wanted it now. And if it meant summoning all her courage to go by herself, so be it.

She had it covered. Sorted!

It felt incredibly empowering to have a plan B. If her friend wasn't available, she would summon the courage to go to the meeting on her own. At least this way, she wouldn't be dependent on external circumstances or whether her friend had time. She had taken control of the situation.

What could possibly go wrong now?

But then...

The handover didn't go as smoothly as planned.

The landlord was unfriendly and treated her in a patronising manner. He never missed an opportunity to show Sarah that he would have preferred to rent his flat to someone else. Sarah's head started spinning as she imagined the worst. What if she didn't get along with her landlord for the next few years? Hell!

Her old feelings of chaos in her head took over again. She briefly realised she was painting a bleak picture of the future, but it was already too late.

Sarah felt off balance and uncomfortable again.

After all the effort she had made to get here on her own! Life wasn't fair!

Just one day later, she fell ill.

A person very close to me shouted at me.
I just replied in a friendly manner.
A day later, I became ill.
It felt like my immune system
took a nose dive ↓

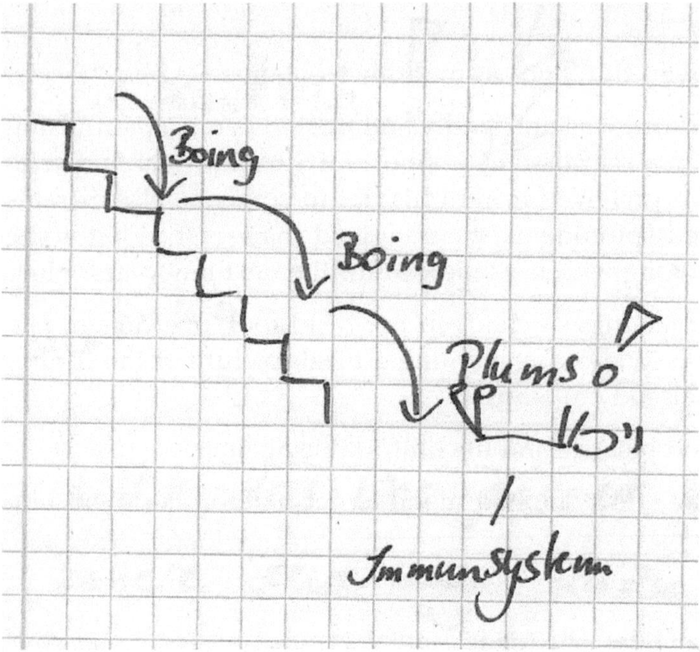

how do I get up again?

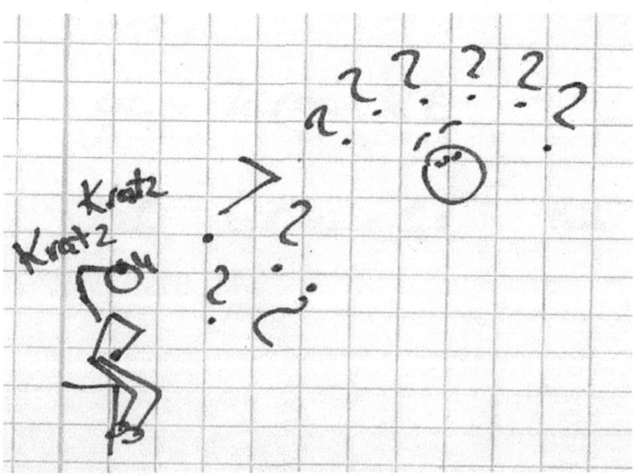

CHAPTER 10 - DEAR OLD BELIEF SYSTEMS

Sarah's head was heavy, making it impossible to think about packing boxes or structuring her day. Frustrated, she collapsed back onto the bed, struggling to fall asleep. She reproached herself, but that did nothing to help her find inner peace.

'Where is my cat when I need her?' she thought.

The familiar purring and gentle kneading of her cat would have soothed her like a warm blanket. Sarah realised she should stay in the present moment instead of letting her mind wander into an uncertain future. She wasn't doing herself any favours by imagining endless conflicts with her landlord. Maybe he had just been having a bad day. After all, everyone is only human.

Just then, her phone rang. It was her grandma, checking in on how the move was going.

'Oh, Grandma,' Sarah sighed. *'I'm sick again.'*

Her grandma's calm and reassuring voice immediately put her at ease. No judgment, no pressure—just unconditional support. With her, Sarah never had to prove anything.

'I've finally started using the methods from your journal, Granny. But I feel like I'm going in circles. I'm stuck.'

Grandma listened patiently, then told her about a holistic approach—one that worked with body, mind, and soul all at once. It had been the key to her own breakthrough.

Any holistic method can be helpful and a turning point. But her grandma specifically told her about tapping acupressure—a technique that used acupressure points on the body to restore balance by lightly tapping on them with the fingertips. No needles—just gentle tapping.

As her grandma explained the method, Sarah recalled that they had tried it together once before. Back then, it had brought her some relief for a few days, but it hadn't really helped in the long run.

'Maybe that's because you haven't yet transformed your old beliefs,' her grandma countered. 'Look, for generations, people in our family carried a kind of **victim mentality**. They sabotaged themselves, felt guilty for one thing or another, and no longer allowed themselves to be happy. It had a lot to do with the war. One day, when we have more time, I'll tell you about it—you'd be surprised how many people still struggle with issues rooted in the First or Second World War, even if they weren't there themselves.

This is called **transgenerational transmission of trauma**. It can even begin in the womb. But explaining all that would take too long right now. Besides, you're ill, dear child. I just wish you a speedy recovery. The most important thing for you to know is this: You can let go of these old patterns—and by doing so, you'll achieve true transformation.'

Her grandmother cautioned her that deep-seated issues or trauma should only be addressed by a qualified doctor or alternative practitioner. Sarah had one more question. Her grandma responded with an example: 'We once had a woman in a workshop who struggled to fully accept her daughter-in-law. It took her a long time to admit that she didn't think the daughter-in-law was 'good enough' for her son. But when she finally said it out loud, without fear of judgment, it was incredibly liberating.'

'But... without being judged?' Sarah asked in disbelief.

'Exactly,' her grandma replied. 'The seminar leader asked us to explore why she couldn't accept her daughter-in-law in the first place. After some reflection, the group discovered that the mother-in-law had never been accepted as a daughter herself—her own mother had always wanted a son, not a girl. Can you imagine? This pain had remained unhealed, and as a result, her soul projected that unresolved hurt onto her daughter-in-law. Nature seeks balance, and the soul often expresses its internal struggles outwardly. This works both ways: we receive emotional burdens, and we pass them on. But the beauty of awareness is that we can heal these wounds, stop passing down these emotional burdens to our children, grandchildren, or others in our lives, and finally break the cycle.'

The workshop group had developed an understanding of the woman, as she had also experienced rejection at a young age. This allowed them to see the situation in a different light and to refrain from passing judgment.

This case had a very happy ending. The woman was able to resolve the old and new family drama with the help of the group, gaining clarity on her own needs.

At the end of the phone call, her grandma offered further help, but Sarah gratefully declined. She had a feeling that she would feel better the next day.

A new idea was gradually taking shape in her mind: she would combine the structured list from her old journal with tapping acupressure!

Back then, when her grandmother wrote the journal, she hadn't known about tapping acupressure points. She had only learned about them later on. If this method had helped her grandma, it gave Sarah the courage and hope that it could work for her too. Her grandma offered to explain the method to her in more detail. It was worth a try!

'Oh wait!' Sarah heard her grandma call to her grandad. 'I need to go back into the house – I've forgotten my denture. Ha ha! Be glad you don't have problems like that, dear Sarah. Get well soon!'

Sarah laughed. 'Nan, what are you like!'

Drop the victim mentality

Recognise old patterns:
(e.g. the accusation: you still owe me)

Reclaim strength & power
by getting it sorted yourself
& taking good care of yourself

Sarah tapped gently on her thymus gland, repeating the phrases: ' I am loved and protected. I am loved and protected. I am loved and protected.'

The rhythmic tapping mimicked the steady beat of a heart: tap, tap, short pause, tap, tap, short pause, and so on. The calming rhythm seemed to ease her mind, and after a while, she felt a noticeable shift. Intuitively, she sensed that this exercise was nurturing her entire being. From that moment on, she made it a regular practice, knowing that repetition would only deepen the positive effects.

The next day, Sarah sat down at the table, pen and paper in hand. Sometimes, it felt as though the Universe was asking: '*So, who wants another pinch of bad luck sprinkled on their life path?*' In the past, Sarah had always seemed to raise her hand, shouting, '*Here! Me! My turn again!*' But not this time. Not anymore. It was time for a change. **From today on, she was committed to focusing only on the good in any given situation. More specifically, she sought to connect with the good energies in each situation—and even in the people she met.**

This new attitude of gratitude felt like a perfect fit for her. She grabbed her journal for inspiration and began to write, determined to shift her perspective once and for all.

Cutting to the Chase

Focus-Sentences:

- Why am I on the path of healing?
- Because I have healed before.
- Because I love myself.
- Because I have a healthy immune system.
- Because I stopped judging me.

Sarah thought, 'I'd better rewrite that in a positive form, since the subconscious speaks in images and doesn't process negations.'

So:

- Why am I on a healing journey?

Because I love and value myself. I embrace and accept myself fully

Then she thought of more 'why' questions:

- why am I resonating with the best (with the divine) of the situation?

Because my focus now is on the positive.

- Why do I feel happy and content?

Because I'm taking good care of myself - because I love myself.

Sarah liked 'why' questions. Everyone has their own individual answers. Her answers were different from her grandmother's.

It was a great tool for self-awareness. **'Why' questions guide the subconscious mind toward positive answers**. They prompt deeper, more reflective responses, helping to focus on the best aspects of any situation. A simple yet powerful way to shift the mindset!

<u>Tapping Sentences: (Sarah used these while tapping the meridian points at the same time)</u>

- Even though I'm afraid of rejection, I still love myself just the way I am.
- I embrace my worries—they are valid and have a purpose.
- What
- These feelings show me where I have an imbalance and what needs healing.

Grandma's advice: **Avoid revealing sentences!**

Only discuss deeply personal or revealing thoughts with an experienced practitioner you trust and feel comfortable with.

After a phone call with her grandmother, Sarah understood the difference between **revealing** and **stabilising** sentences. It made sense to focus on affirmations that strengthened the subconscious.

Step one: Become aware of where exactly the problem lies. **Step two:** Use stabilising sentences to regain balance.

Healing the Mother Wound

Whatever I lack in basic trust, I will give to myself—love, understanding, unwavering support, and nourishment in every way.
I will connect with Mother Earth and the universe.
I imagine my loving ancestors standing behind me, sending their love from wherever they are.
I allow positive energy to flow through me and heal the mother wound.

Every now and then, they needed a break. Her grandma reminded her of their courage-building dance. To the tune of their favourite song, they sang: 'I can do anything! Youuhuhu, yeah, I can do anything! I'm so good—oh yes, I am!' Whatever playful lyrics came to mind, they sang with gusto. A little dance, and she felt elated for a while. Laughing and dancing, her grandma gently reminded her: ***'Wholehearted love drives out fear.'***

Then Sarah sat down again and reflected on the next question in the journal: *'What exactly is bothering me about the current situation?'*

- Why am I able to bring peace into this situation?
- Why does God or the Universe bring peace to the situation?
- Why is peace present in this situation?

She quickly jotted down whatever came to her mind.

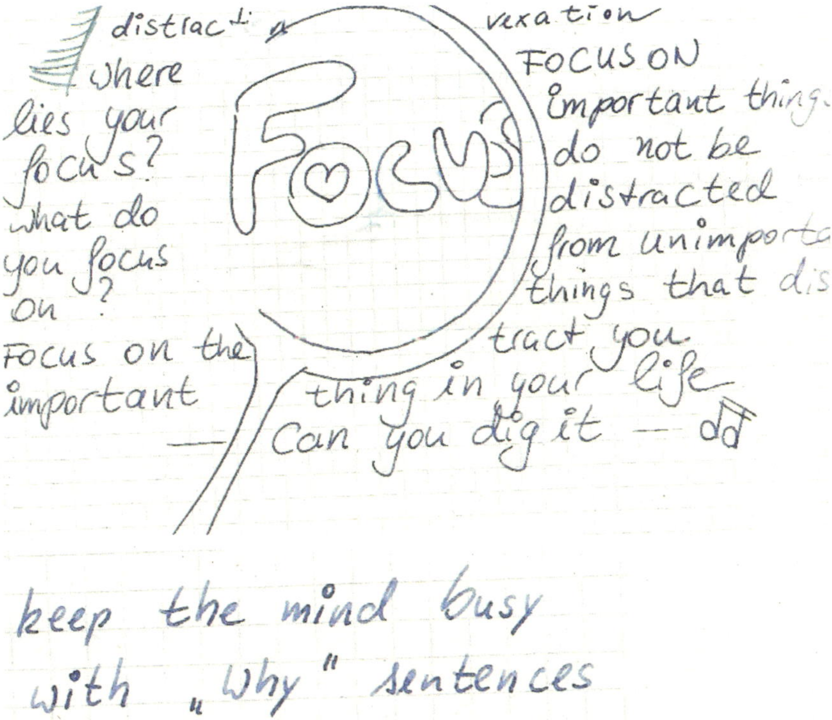

Learning by Doing – Stay Focused!

'*Why*' questions matter – more than '*how*' questions. If I were to ask, '*How can I bring peace to this situation?*' my critical mind might respond with, '*Not at all.*' But '*why*' questions create a positive environment for the desired outcome, helping to bypass overthinking and self-doubt.

Whenever intellectual doubt starts creeping in, this method can help keep you on track.

I am thankful for:

- ______________________
- ______________________

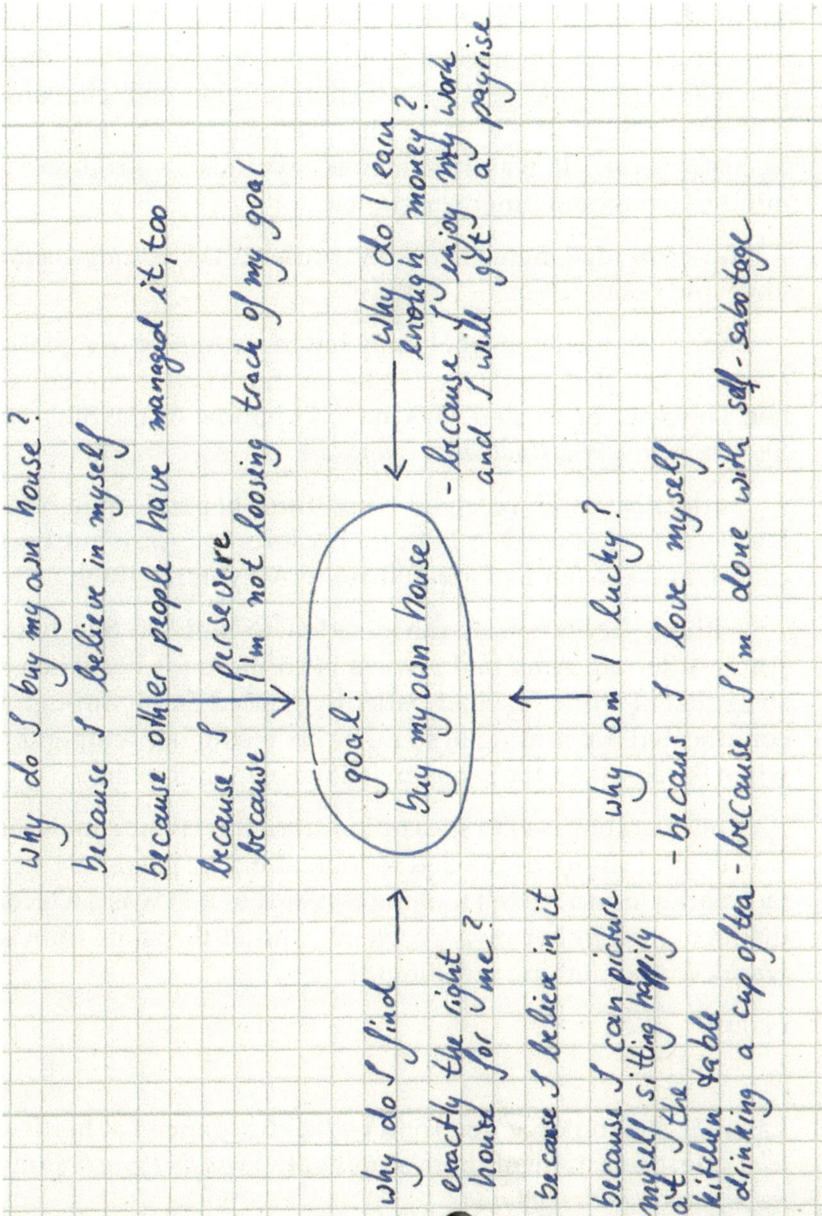
why do I buy my own house?
because I believe in myself
because other people have managed it, too
because I persevere
because I'm not loosing track of my goal
goal: buy my own house
why do I earn enough money?
- because I enjoy my work and I will get a payrise
why am I lucky?
- because I love myself
- because I'm done with self-sabotage
why do I find exactly the right house for me?
because I believe in it
because I can picture myself sitting happily at the kitchen table drinking a cup of tea

Sarah decided to adopt this method for finding solutions, believing it could be applied to any goal she set for herself. She planned to personalize it by incorporating her own challenges, rephrasing them in a way that her subconscious would accept as instructions. It was like mental gymnastics—training her mind to **overcome inner resistance**.

She reminded herself to stay present. *What truly matters?* Love and connection.

She envisioned herself already having achieved her goal and asked, *What emotions do I feel?* She let those joyful emotions fill her. The rest, she trusted, was in God's hands. As the Bible says: *Imagine you have already achieved it.*

Suddenly, Sarah received a text from her colleague Nicole. Nicole was supposed to help their coworker Amy but had to cancel, and she felt bad about leaving Amy in the lurch.

Without hesitation, Sarah decided to step in. She felt for Amy—after all, Amy had always been there for her when she struggled at work. She had patiently guided Sarah through the complicated accounting system, never losing her temper, even when Sarah asked the same questions over and over.

Now, Sarah was glad she could return the favor. Amy's mom was ill, and someone needed to look after her pets. *Easy job!* In fact, Sarah found herself looking forward to it. It was a welcome distraction from her own problems, and at the same time, she was doing something meaningful.

Perfect!

Later, as she took the dog for a walk, she glanced at her list of *why* **questions. One of them stood out:** *'Why do I find healing for the situation with my mum?'*

As she walked, she repeated the question out loud several times. Deep in the forest, she paused, inhaling the crisp air. A profound sense of tranquility washed over her.

Suddenly, a deep calm settled within her, and she realized that the solution was already within her consciousness. It became clear—she was no longer dependent on her mother's behavior toward her. The key lay in her own perception, her own interpretation of things.

Once again, it all came down to **awareness**.

She realized that the feeling of being uprooted wasn't just tied to her relationship with her mother—it ran much deeper. It was a sense of disconnection from her core, from her basic confidence and trust. Perhaps, she thought, it even stemmed from a feeling of being detached from her primordial consciousness.

Maybe it was something she had experienced in her childhood, but now, as an adult, she wondered: *Could she heal this on her own?*

At that moment, rays of sunlight broke through the clouds, as if the heavens were answering her. Sarah couldn't help but giggle, feeling the warm sunlight dance across her face.

be in the here & now

CHAPTER 12 - APPEASING THE EGO

Sarah often found herself tempted to wallow in her suffering. In her mind, a noble knight in shining armor would appear at her door, ready to fulfill all her deepest desires. This hero could rescue her from the abyss of meaninglessness, relieving her of any worry or responsibility. If something went wrong, she could hold her head high and confidently say, "*I would have done it better.*" Just like she always did before.

But deep down, Sarah knew that this old pattern no longer fit her.

The desire to blame her ex for the situation was strong. After all, it was his fault she was in this mess, so surely, he should help her get out of it. A part of her believed he still owed her this. Sometimes, she felt like shouting at him: 'Look how bad I feel! Now, do something about it!'

The thought of handing over responsibility to someone else was tempting. But, upon reflection, she realized that this would leave her feeling just as helpless, powerless, and lost as before. She'd be dependent on someone else again. No, thank you.

It wouldn't truly help if her ex showed up just because of a guilty conscience. That would only provide short-term relief and feed her ego. A flattered ego might feel good for a while, but she had read enough about the ego trap to know this wasn't the answer. In the long run, those fleeting positive feelings wouldn't last. It didn't feel right. If someone only acted out of guilt, it never felt genuine. And, she thought, she certainly wouldn't want to be manipulated this way either.

If I treat others the way I want to be treated, I won't create new karma or drama. Instead, I'll focus on what's best for everyone involved.

I choose to let go of the thought that my ex still owes me something. What a revelation!

That doesn't mean I have to forget everything. On a soul level, I can forgive – but in my daily life, I will set healthy boundaries.

She recalled the advice she had given her colleague: *'Don't interfere in other people's affairs or family matters. Otherwise, you give them permission to interfere in yours.'*

It was so easy to give good advice to others.

She sighed, then flipped through her journal, hoping to distract herself.

how do I keep fear in check?

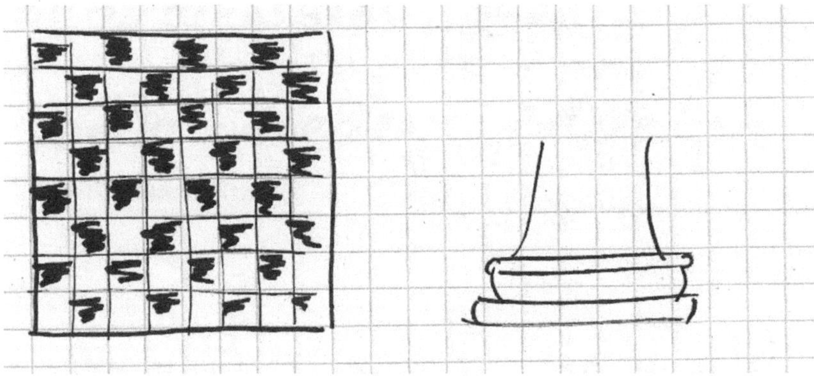

by your thoughts + feelings

walk through fear:
what do I need?

5 elements:

air - breathe
water - drink
earth - to provide + earth/grounding
fire - energy, inner fire, warmth
spirit - focus & spiritual connection
& LOVE

Master your Mind

By now, Sarah was used to her Granny's scrawl and could decipher it with increasing ease. Quite a challenge!

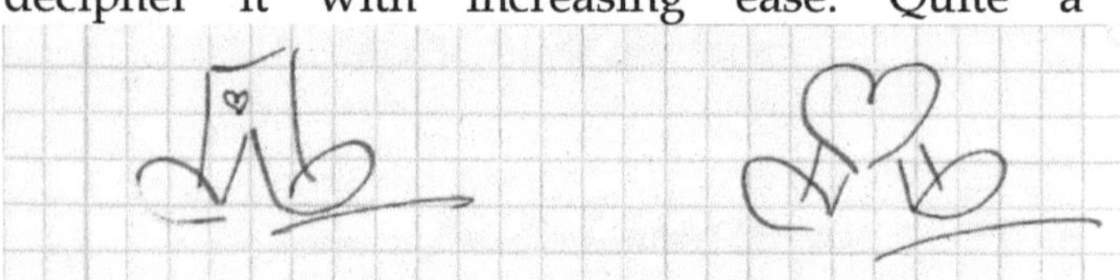

When your heart is in your boots -

make sure your ♥ stands on its own feet again!

Sarah was desperate for a break.

Quick Ritual:

'I'll go into the forest and leave my worries behind.'

Even as a child, she had often wandered into the woods, confiding in the trees, unburdening her heart. It always amazed her how refreshing a simple walk in nature could be. And when she added a small ritual, the relief felt even greater.

That day, she asked her angels for guidance. Intuitively, she shared her troubles with the stones in her hand, then gently placed them beside a patch of deep green moss. Mother Earth will recycle and renew them, she thought.

'I'll let go of my old problems and focus on what I truly want instead,' she reminded herself—feeling lighter already.

Sarah took a few moments to sit on the soft grass, inhaling deeply. The crisp forest air felt invigorating, filling her lungs with freshness and calm. It didn't take long before she drifted into a deep state of relaxation.

She then chose a new mantra: *'I thank the Universe for this wonderful opportunity to move into a great flat.'* Closing her eyes, she **visualized her desire as if it had already come true**. She committed to repeating this affirmation for at least 21 days.

After a while, she felt recharged, her energy renewed. With a contented sigh, she stood up, ready to return to her day.

Feeling elated, she headed back to her tasks – there were still a few boxes left to pack!

Transformation: From self-sabotage in the morning to heroic deeds by evening.

All it took was a short break to recharge her energy.

Sarah called her grandma with the happy news that she was feeling much better.

Her grandma responded with a knowing tone. 'People go to a seminar and feel on top of the world for a while. But tell me, how long do you think that feeling lasts?'

Sarah paused to think before replying, 'I don't know... a year?'

Her grandma chuckled. 'Oh, dear Sarah, if only! Most of the time, those good intentions and the motivation to change fade after just a few weeks. People get caught up in their daily routines, and when they have to change more than one old habit at a time, they quickly feel overwhelmed.'

'I can sympathize with that,' Sarah replied. 'Especially for people like me, who need their old rhythm to feel safe.'

'Yes, of course, my dear,' her grandma responded. 'But if we want change, we can't keep doing things the same way. The power to change is within us. If we relinquish responsibility, we become dependent on others – on what they do or don't do.'

'True,' Sarah sighed.

Take charge of what truly matters to you, **key themes close to your heart**

Grandma was on a roll. 'If you accept and understand your situation, then you are not resisting your current position. That is important. When you surrender to the situation and to life, your body and symptoms are showing you exactly what you need to see right now. All the good reasons for it. If you accept or surrender to the situation, it becomes easier to understand or transform it, rather than being in constant resistance to what is.'

'Whether it's 'low tide in your bank account,' being in an 'unhealthy relationship,' or suffering from other symptoms, these are all expressions that you're not in the flow, but in a state of lack. The following thought helped me a lot:

'All good reasons for the current situation.'

It helped me have faith and build trust.'

'If you want to get rid of the inner saboteur or victim mentality, it's important to fill that void with something else,' Grandma explained. 'For example, we might have a systemic connection or link.'

'What is a systemic link?' Sarah asked.

'It's a **generational pattern or unconscious bond.** Imagine that, unconsciously, we took on the role of the victim through a loved one when we were young. For instance, a daughter might internalize it from her mother. Unconsciously, we might say, 'I'll do it like you, Mum,' or 'I'll do it like you, Dad.' The bond with a beloved family member is very strong. It's important to replace this bond with something positive before letting go of the negative pattern. That way, the subconscious can release the old pattern. Otherwise, it might not be possible, as the deep attachment could be too strong.'

I once had a friend, and together we replaced an old bond with a positive, connecting pattern. I asked her, *'What wonderful memory do you have of your mum?'* For her, it was gardening. So, she planted a new flower and lovingly remembered her beloved mother.

In replacing the pattern of '*victim mentality*' with the new pattern of '*flower love,*' she transformed the old habit. The new bond was infused with the love of flowers, which gently reminded her of her mother. This new attachment was nurtured in her thoughts and feelings, and the subconscious was finally able to release the victim mentality.

Why? Because no conflicting belief stood in its way. Previously, the belief was: **'I must hold on to this old pattern that reminds me of my mother, or that connects me to her.'** And just imagine, dear Sarah, after that, she was able to let go of the victim mentality. Healing could finally take place. Everything she set her mind to became much more successful. Every time she tended to her flowers, she remembered her beloved mum, and the unconscious self-sabotage stopped once and for all.

'That sounds amazing,' Sarah said. 'But how do you get rid of the victim mentality?'

stop saying 'no'
before someone else does

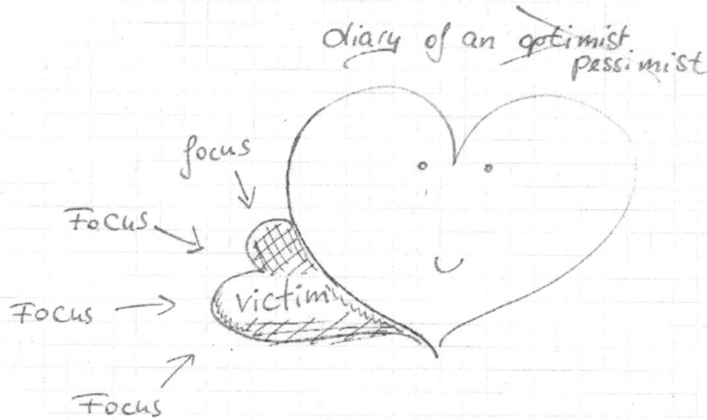

In a victim mentality, the focus is on the internal judgment that '*something went wrong.*' But who can say, in the long run, whether what happened was a hidden blessing or not? After all, growth and awareness often come from a variety of experiences. Sometimes, it's even helpful when one door closes because another one can open.

There can also be hidden advantages to holding onto a victim mentality. It keeps you comfortably in your comfort zone. Others may step in to comfort you when things go wrong, and you have a certain place in the family dynamic. Who knows if you would still be loved or accepted if you were more successful than the current 'number one' in the family? That might shake the entire family structure.

Once you recognize how the victim mentality may serve certain purposes or provide perceived benefits, it can become easier to release yourself from that role. These advantages might be helpful for a time, but at some point in your life, they will no longer serve you.

What would I advise my best friend? To embrace happiness! And I can do that too. I'm allowed to embrace happiness as well.

When nothing seems to work, and your mind has fallen into a victim mentality, try to imagine yourself being supported by your ancestors. Picture them standing behind you, sending you heartfelt blessings of luck and strength.

Sarah was lost in thought when her grandma continued, 'There are many ways to shed a victim mentality.'

'Sometimes, it can be as simple as burning a piece of paper. You can create a small ritual – write down what you want to let go of, then offer it to the fire. The act of burning is a powerful symbol of release. Just as the fire transforms paper into ashes, you, too, can transform and release old energy.'

'Ultimately, it comes down to a conscious choice – a decision to align yourself with all the good the universe has to offer. A choice to shift your focus. To turn your attention toward something new.'

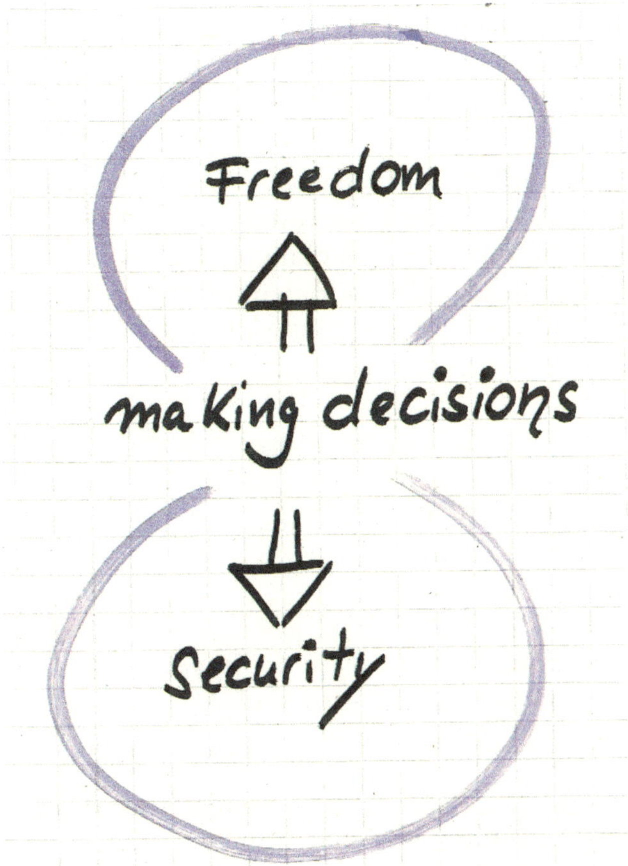

Can you have both – freedom and security?

Yes, as long as your decisions are based on love.

"Some people get tired of constant positive thinking. This can be a sign that it's time to look for the 'good' within the 'negative'—in other words, to integrate the shadow. It's about understanding the deeper reasons behind the inner saboteur."

"A good example of this is secondary gain from illness. You may be sick and worried about your future, but at the same time, a part of you might feel relieved that you don't have to go to work. That's the hidden 'benefit' within the 'negative' situation. Recognizing these hidden gains is the first step before truly transforming the victim mentality."

'You see, my dear, we are body, mind, and soul. But what do you think came first?'

'Mmmh,' Sarah pondered. 'The soul?'

'Well, that's probably a question everyone must answer for themselves... But yes, I think so too—the soul...'

Just then, her cat Amruk trotted over, pining for attention.

'And if the soul came first,' Grandma continued, 'then it must have chosen our parents and our bodies, don't you think?'

Sarah's eyes widened.

'And that,' Grandma mused, 'is perhaps our greatest task in life—to **accept our lot and then transform it**. To forgive the mistakes our parents made and, in time, **to forgive ourselves**. Maybe we needed all these external struggles to finally **find the solution within**.'

Sarah frantically stroked her cat, trying to let it all sink in.

'I am who I am because of my experiences,' she thought—

'both good and bad.'

The realization brought her an unexpected sense of peace.

'You won't believe this!' Grandma chirped. 'Grandpa has a work waistcoat with Velcro fasteners to secure the pockets. One day, he was about to head out shopping when, by pure chance, I noticed something stuck to his waistcoat—a pair of ladies' knickers! They must have clung to the Velcro in the last wash.'

'You should have seen him!' she continued, chuckling. 'Strutting around the kitchen, completely unaware, proudly showcasing those briefs! I laughed my head off. It took him ages to realize what was going on. Imagine if I'd let him walk through the supermarket like that!'

Sarah burst out laughing, gasping for air. Thank heavens for her Grandparents she thought. They were truly one of a kind.

CHAPTER 14 - A CLARIFYING CONVERSATION

Time and again, Sarah found herself slipping back into old patterns of melancholy. Worrying about an uncertain future, she imagined the worst possible outcomes. During the day, she felt fine, distracted by her tasks. But in the evening, as soon as darkness fell, her fears crept back in, wrapping around her like a heavy fog. She didn't know how to move forward.

It didn't help that she kept comparing herself to others—successful, confident people who seemed to have it all figured out. In their shadow, she felt small, unimportant, and utterly stuck. She knew her grandma was just a phone call away, always ready with words of wisdom, but she couldn't call her every time she felt low. She had to learn how to navigate these moments on her own.

Now and then, Sarah simply lost momentum. What truly mattered right now?

She recalled her grandma's advice: 'When you read something from the journal, you'll **intuitively feel what resonates with you**. Maybe you'll get goosebumps. Or perhaps you're drawn to a particular topic. Whatever it is—that's what matters to you right now.'

'Okay, I've faced my fears,' Sarah thought. 'So why are they still here?'

Her exasperated thoughts were suddenly interrupted by the sound of a key turning in the lock. Moments later, the sharp clack of high heels echoed down the hallway. Sarah's door was still wide open.

'Oh no – she'll see me with tears in my eyes.'

Sarah tensed. The last thing she wanted was for her father's girlfriend to catch her in a vulnerable moment. She refused to give this power woman the satisfaction of seeing her at her weakest. But it was already too late.

'Hello!' Andrea called out cheerfully.

Ever since Sarah had announced her moving date, Andrea's behavior had shifted – completely. It was as if she had done a full 180. Clearly, she was relieved that Sarah was leaving.

Standing in the doorway, Andrea studied Sarah for a moment.

'What's the matter, sweetie? Hey, come here!'

Sarah could have done without the sweetie, but Andrea's voice was warm, her expression surprisingly kind.

Sarah looked up, wary. 'You don't have time to listen to me anyway.'

'Hey, I've got time now,' Andrea said, stepping inside. 'I'm sorry if we didn't get off to the best start. Back then, I wasn't sure where things stood with your father. I was afraid he wouldn't want me here anymore when you moved back in. And honestly, I worried he'd want to spend a lot more time with you – maybe even instead of me.'

She sighed before continuing. 'But now, I see that's not the case. He did mention wanting to do things alone with you sometimes, and that's perfectly fine. I understand now. After all, I don't always want him around either – especially on a girls' night out!'

Andrea smiled and tilted her head. 'So, if you'd like, I'll just take off my shoes and sit with you for a few minutes.'

Sarah hesitated for a moment. She had made a firm promise to herself—to take better care of her well-being. Did that mean shielding herself from a conversation with Andrea in case it unsettled her?

She met Andrea's gaze. Her expression was open, her demeanor warm. There was no sign of the tension that had once existed between them.

Sarah took a deep breath. Maybe I don't have to shut this down. Maybe I can just meet her where she is.

With that thought, she decided to mirror Andrea's friendliness and nodded. 'Okay. Let's have a heart-to-heart.'

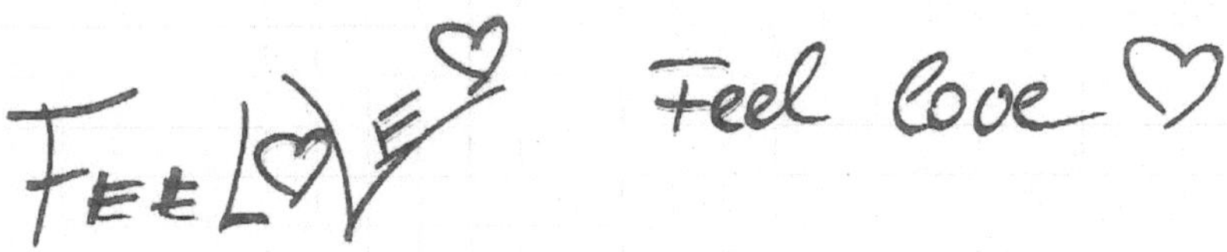

The conversation with Andrea had done her good. Sarah was relieved that she hadn't brushed her off or snapped back with a snotty remark, like she might have in the past. That would have only shut down any chance for understanding.

In the end, they even raised their lemonade glasses. Andrea smiled and offered the old toast: '*Never above you, never below you – always beside you.*' As she spoke, she lifted her glass above Sarah's, then below, before finally clinking it at the same level.

Sarah felt honored. But more than that—she felt seen and understood. And that, above all, felt good.

It was reassuring to know that she could talk to Andrea even when her father wasn't around. Their conversation had given her a sense of ease.

Feeling lighter, Sarah took a deep breath, pulled herself together, and got back to tidying up.

Beforehand, she glanced at her notes.

Even though her mind wasn't quite ready to accept it, her new mantra had a remarkable effect: *I connect with the good in the present situation.*

It brought her a sense of calm. Surrendering to the here and now, she realised there was no need to resist the current moment. After all, it was giving her space to rediscover herself.

CHAPTER 15 - BETWEEN POWER QUESTIONS AND MANTRAS

In the evening, Sarah was too tired for anything strenuous. She settled into her chair and absentmindedly flicked through her grandma's journal. As always, it was filled with wisdom, and one passage on **perseverance** caught her eye.

Sometimes, just when you're ready to let go of something, it seems to push back even harder. That's when it's important to accept it first—**completely surrender to the present moment**. No judgment. No resistance. Just an acknowledgment of 'it is what it is.' Only then can you **refocus on what you truly want**.

Something in those words ignited a spark in Sarah. Suddenly, she couldn't rest until she had written everything down.

A surge of determination washed over her. No more hesitation. She grabbed her Focus List and, with a fire in her heart, added a few more points. Finally, she was ready to jump through the hoop.

judge not <=> you won't be judged

(And don't judge yourself either – but if you do, let it be with love. See it as gentle self-reflection, a kind evaluation, not harsh criticism.)

This time, Sarah was determined to get to the heart of it.

- Why do I manage to remain level-headed?
- Why do I succeed in moving flats with ease and grace?
- Why am I feeling grateful today?
- Why am I feeling happy today?

She paused and decided to refine the last sentence:

- Why do I feel fullfilled today?

At first, not all of the questions were immediately answered by her subconscious. But after a round of tapping, she wrote down the insights that came to her mind.

- Why do I manage to keep a clear head?

Because I remain at peace.

Because I've done it before.

- Why do I succeed in moving flats with ease and grace?

Because I believe in myself.

Because I am supported.

- Why do I speak my mind without feeling bad about it?

Because it's my turn to express myself with ease.

- Why am I feeling gratitude today?

Because I focus on what I'm grateful for.

- Why am I feeling fulfilled and happy today?

Because I feel loved.

Because I love myself.

Because I feel good.

Because I enjoy my favourite food.

Because I can create happy emotions.

I am loved.

I am grateful.

I give my emotions a home within myself.

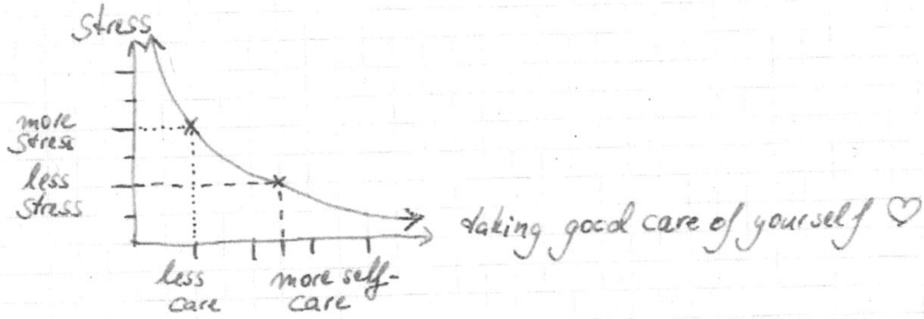

She wondered if it really could be that easy sometimes. Yes, it could be as simple as enjoying her favorite food or listening to her favorite music—just generating happy moments. Why make life more complicated than it already was?

That day, Sarah focused on the **here and now**, and one by one, her old negative belief systems fell like dominoes.

"Indigenous people understand the importance of transforming stress and fear. Many hold festivals where they dance to the point of ecstasy—a state that, when used correctly, has been reporeted to bring profound benefits. But with or without natural ecstasy, our feelings play a crucial role. Following pleasant emotions, both for ourselves and others, can be a powerful way to reprogram the subconscious."

I love this **mantra** from the journal:

How do I feel after my desired outcome has manifested?

How do I feel when I have received what I truly want?

It is essential to visualise this and deeply immerse yourself in the feeling—to fully experience the joy, relief, satisfaction, and all the other positive emotions that come with it.

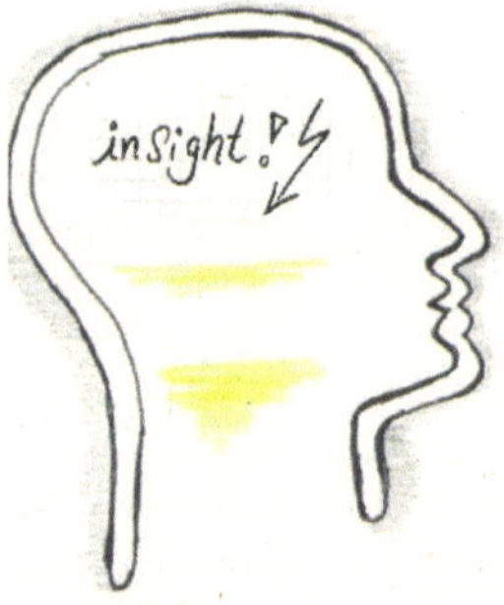

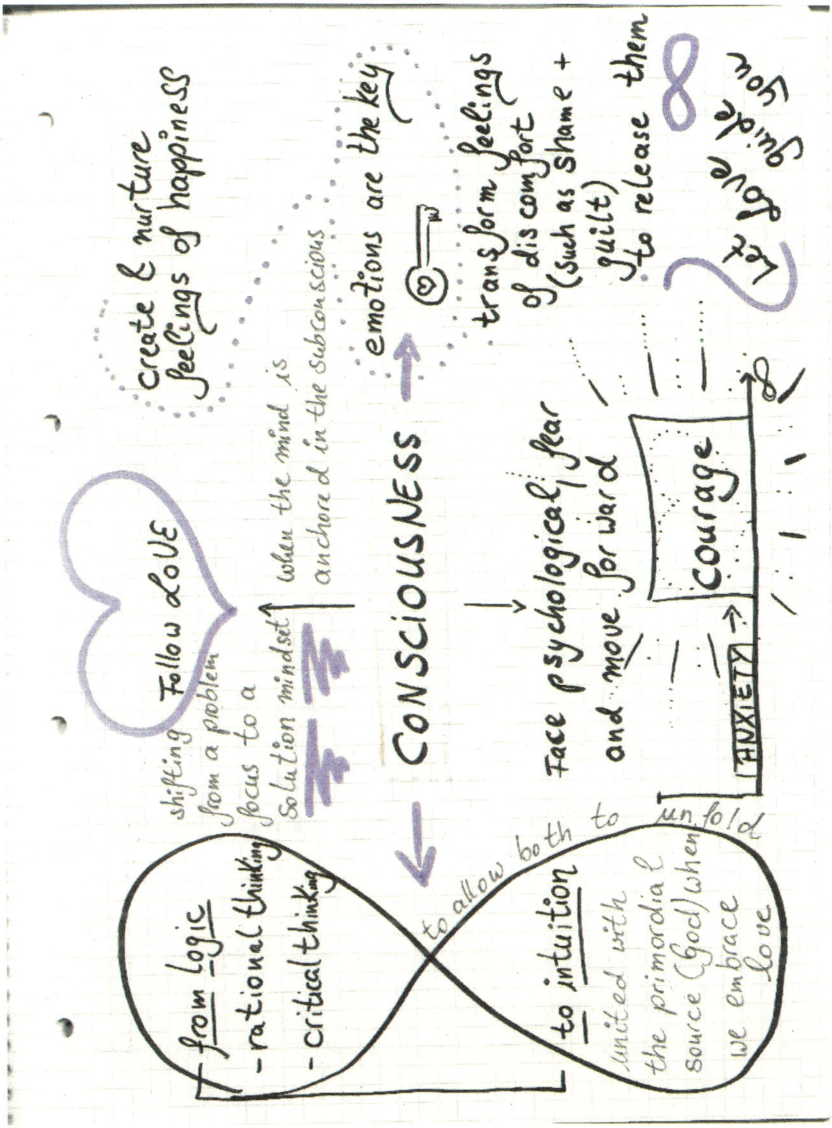

from logic
- rational thinking
- critical thinking
to intuition
united with the primordial source (God) when we embrace love
to allow both to unfold
shifting from a problem focus to a solution mindset
Follow LOVE
when the mind is anchored in the subconscious
CONSCIOUSNESS
create & nurture feelings of happiness
emotions are the key
transform feelings of discomfort (such as shame + guilt) to release them
Face psychological fear and move forward
ANXIETY
Courage
Let love guide you

"It all comes down to motivation: Love or fear?

Am I acting out of lack, or from a place of love and trust? And how do I recognize which one it is?

Every decision I make—am I choosing from a mindset of scarcity, or from confidence and trust? Sometimes, motivations are a mix of different emotions, and that's where awareness becomes crucial. What were the driving forces behind my decision? Were they rooted in fear and insecurity, or in faith that everything will work out?

By recognizing this, we can restore a healthy balance when making future choices. Mothers of multiple children know this well—you can't always please everyone at the same time."

Sarah found herself deeply intrigued by the topic of motivation. Suddenly, things made more sense. She realized that the key to success might lie in this simple truth:

Are you acting out of fear, or out of trust?"

Keep my focus on what I want.
(not on what I want to avoid)

Confucius allegedly said, **"The journey is its own reward."**

What motivates me to walk this path? It's the *how* that counts—not necessarily where or when.

The journey is its own reward...

Not just the journey's destination—this takes the pressure off and allows you to focus on the here and now. In this way, you remain open to your truth and connected to the natural flow.

Deep within, she felt the truth—wholehearted love drives out fear.

It doesn't really matter what your goal is; it's more about the *how*, not just the *what*.

How do you approach it?

With love?

With inner peace?

By being fully present in the here and now?

You are already at home—you just have to remember.

Sarah resolved to feel more at home in her own body:

I am whole and complete just as I am—body, mind, and soul, she whispered to herself.

SUCCESS

SUCCESS
is about allowing things to succeed.
Align with what unfolds
embrace positive emotions
By cultivating gratitude, we anchor joy
& learn to appreciate the
little things that make
life meaningful x

She took a closer look at the concept of success and what it truly meant. Why were material possessions so highly valued in society? Wasn't one successful if they had done something meaningful for a neighbor? Weren't you successful if you had organized a memorable birthday party? Wasn't that what truly mattered in life? The moments and memories you created along the way.

As she continued reading the booklet, one sentence caught her eye:

"To be successful means to be in harmony with what happens."

What a realization—if that was the true measure of success, then she was successful almost every day!

CHAPTER 16 - MOTHERLOVE

The phone rang, and Sarah was surprised to see her mum's profile on the screen.

'Hello, my darling,' her mum's warm voice greeted her. 'I wanted to get in touch. I'll be in Germany soon and I'd love to visit you in your new flat.'

After a while, her mum's tone shifted, and she asked, 'Has your father given you the box with your old letters yet?'

Sarah was caught off guard. 'No, he hasn't,' she replied.

Her mum sighed softly. 'Sarah, then I have to tell you something. Your father didn't have the courage to tell you for a long time. His ex-girlfriend didn't pass on most of the letters I wrote to you when you were a child. Your father said that she was probably afraid he would come to Thailand too, because I had invited you every year during the summer holidays.'

She paused before continuing. 'I don't know why she thought that. I would've found another way to get you here. Grandma could have flown over with you, or I could have come to pick you up. It was all a mess and so complicated. Your father and I barely spoke at the time.'

Sarah was left stunned, processing the weight of her mother's words.

And all those years, Sarah had thought that her mum had simply stopped contacting her. The truth was that her father's ex-girlfriend had never forwarded her mum's letters. How was that even possible? Sarah's mind spun, trying to make sense of it all. Then, a memory surfaced: her mum had occasionally asked her on the phone if she wanted to come to Thailand. At the time, Sarah had dismissed it as a joke and hadn't thought much of it.

'Sarah,' her mum's voice broke through her thoughts, 'please never forget that I love you. Some really bad things happened back then, and I'm so sorry. I was the adult and I should've taken care of things. But please, don't just reduce me to my mistakes. You and I had good times, too, and you know that! All I can do now is apologise. You were just a child, and you didn't understand the problems between your father and me.'

Her mum's voice softened, 'I just want you to know that I have always loved you and always will. Your dad found the box with my old letters and told grandma about it. I don't know why he hasn't given it to you yet... maybe he just forgot. Please, give me a big hug. I look forward to seeing you very soon!'

Sarah was left holding the phone, her heart full of emotions. She felt a wave of both relief and sadness. So many years of unanswered questions suddenly made sense, but the weight of the past was still heavy.

Sarah was still surprised. It took her a while to realise that she might have wronged her mother. Her mum's words were still echoing in her mind: 'Don't reduce me to my mistakes!' And that was exactly what Sarah had done.

She resolved to create a loving environment for herself moving forward, regardless of whether she felt loved or not. She understood that her fellow human beings were just that—human. People make mistakes, just as she could make mistakes herself. After all, no one is perfect.

Later that evening, Sarah distracted herself with social media. She was surprised to come across an article by Mina Bissell, a researcher in biology and cancer studies. Bissell concluded that the key factor in whether cancer could take root was the environment in which it was trying to grow. 'So, it's the environment that determines whether the disease can take hold or not!' thought Sarah. Once again, it seemed to be all about the environment. Interesting.

In the past, her grandma had raised an important question: 'Do you love yourself the way you are?' 'No,' Sarah had replied at the time. There were still parts of her that couldn't fully believe this statement. Instead of staying in a state of deprivation, she chose to shift her focus. Now, she focused on the result she wanted instead. So Sarah tapped:

Why do I love myself the way I am?
I'm only human. And it's human to make mistakes.
Love is unconditional.
I love myself the way I am because I'm a wonderful human being.

Nevertheless, there were still some issues that fueled her self-doubt. The phrase: 'I love myself completely. Just as I am' still didn't feel real and remained just a phrase. How could she truly feel it 100%? Intuitively, she had an idea of how to address this differently. She needed to bypass the critical mind. Don't let doubt seep in.

Generate the emotion, and in doing so, create the vibration to match what she wanted. 'I am happy! I think I'll have a holistic massage and use positive mantras of happiness and bliss. I'll bypass the critical mind to reach the subconscious! Yes, that's it!'

Sarah recalled a passage in the book about suppressed feelings. If you find yourself unable to feel fully, there is always a reason behind it. Instead of resisting, you can choose to accept the present moment—including all the valid reasons for your emotional numbness. Perhaps your subconscious is trying to protect you, or there's a deeper, unacknowledged fear. Maybe part of you resists letting go or forgiving because it feels like doing so would diminish the significance of what happened or make you appear weak. Whatever the reason, it's important not to force emotions but to trust your intuition and allow yourself the time and space to process them naturally.

A few days later, she had her massage appointment. She noticed how the tension in her shoulders gradually lifted. After a while, her whole body began to relax more and more. As the endorphins and other happy hormones flooded her system, she repeated: 'I love myself as I am. With all my heart.' And this time, it really sank in. Deep breaths, slow exhales. Later, she thought that she could do the same during yoga sessions or while walking through the woods. The critical mind would be distracted by the fresh, healthy forest air, and she could deepen her new, positive attitude towards life.

Focus on what I want ★
(not on what holds me back)

CHAPTER 17 - BODY OR MIND?

Sarah decided to seal the deal with a ritual.

She made a pact with herself to focus on the good things from now on. „Where attention goes, energy flows“, wasn't this a famous saying?

However, if she was honest, things didn't always go as smoothly as she had hoped. With each setback, the day of the actual move grew closer. But Sarah stuck to her decisions. The small disappointments only confirmed that she now knew exactly what she wanted. If something mattered enough to disappoint her, it was a clear sign of her true desires.

As a result, she made a new commitment to herself: to do things on her own when necessary, to ensure they got done. Or, she would **practice patience** until her goal was achieved. Most importantly, she was learning to decide what was truly important—the things that would bring her happiness and keep her healthy. This allowed her to be there for the people around her as well—for a new sense of togetherness. But that was only possible if her own batteries were fully charged.

Taking some time for herself, Sarah settled into her favourite armchair. She squeezed the accupressure point on the side of her hand, gently pressing and holding it firmly. The EFT point at the side of the hand. As she hummed her favourite tune, she began to feel a shift within her. Her breathing slowed, becoming deeper and more relaxed.

'I let go immediately and on all levels of everything that doesn't belong to me and doesn't serve my higher self,' she whispered to herself, allowing the peace to wash over her.

Old sayings from teachers or relatives came to Sarah's mind—words she had taken deeply to heart as a child or young adult. Some of these sayings had held her back, but now, by recognizing them, she was setting herself on a new path. She repeated to herself: *'I embrace everything that aligns with me and supports my higher self, releasing all else with ease.'*

As she did, she felt her shoulders relax. She allowed herself the time to fully absorb this shift until a sense of peace settled within her. Sarah decided that whenever she felt down in the future, she would press this pressure point lightly, using it as a kinesthetic anchor, reminding her body that it had the power to restore its own calm.

After this practice, Sarah found it easier to focus on what truly mattered to her.

Sarah wanted to furnish her new flat in a way that made her feel completely at home. After all, there's no better feeling than feeling loved and truly settled. Being surrounded by familiar, beloved things. But what made her feel at home? For Sarah, it was her cats. She adored Amruk and Phaedrus. She had inherited Phaedrus from a motorcyclist who had planned a tour across America and needed temporary care for his cat. But he never returned to reclaim him—and probably never would. Both cats gave her a deep sense of home. Perhaps it was tied to memories from childhood. Whenever she was with them, waves of light-hearted nostalgia washed over her. A simple cat cuddle, and all her worries faded away. Sarah had always been drawn to cats. She believed that everyone should find whatever it is that makes them feel truly at home.

And that sense of home could be different for everyone. The key was to remember what truly made you feel comfortable, safe, and at ease.

The body, too, could recall the feeling of home—often through scents. Hadn't everyone experienced that sudden rush of nostalgia triggered by a familiar smell? The aroma of freshly baked bread, a particular brand of soap, or the scent of an old book could transport you back in time, unlocking memories buried deep in your subconscious.

But if the body could store positive memories through scent, could it also hold onto negative experiences the same way? Sarah suddenly wondered. What if difficult moments from the past—like an unsettling experience at school—were also imprinted somewhere deep within? Could a certain smell, a place, or even a specific atmosphere unknowingly bring back those buried emotions?

The thought intrigued her. It made sense that just as the body responded to comforting, familiar sensations, it might also react to past hardships.

Sarah could still vividly recall a terrible incident from her school days. She had felt bullied and unfairly treated by her teacher, trapped in a situation where she no longer wanted to play along. The worst part was that the teacher himself didn't follow the very rules he so strictly enforced on the rest of the class. A teacher should set an example—but instead, he had humiliated her in front of everyone.

It was so unfair. A surge of disappointment, anger, and sadness had washed over her all at once. The weight of the experience had stayed with her long after that day, even manifesting physically. She had fallen ill soon after.

Years later, as an adult, she had to return to those school grounds for a brief visit. The moment she stepped onto the premises, an unsettling sensation crept over her. A heaviness settled in her chest, and her stomach churned. Though the event itself was long past, the emotions it had stirred still lingered, hidden within her.

Had her body stored the memories associated with that building? Was there a deeper connection, a lingering imprint of past negativity tied to that place? Sarah couldn't shake the thought. Could it be that her body had internalized the emotional impact, linking it to the physical environment?

She recalled a conversation with a colleague who had struggled with hay fever since the fourth grade. Coincidentally, she too had experienced an upsetting incident with a teacher. Sarah began to wonder – what if that incident had taken place in May, right in the middle of pollen season? Could the subconscious mind, in an attempt to protect her from similar distress in the future, have developed an allergy as a defense mechanism? What if the pollen itself had never been the real problem, but rather a substitute – an innocent bystander in a much deeper, emotional response?

It was an intriguing idea, one Sarah wanted to explore further. She made a mental note to ask her colleague if she remembered when exactly that childhood event had occurred. Perhaps it had indeed happened in springtime.

But then another thought crossed her mind. If negative experiences could be anchored in this way, perhaps she could also rewire these associations. Just as she intentionally surrounded herself with things that made her feel at home, could she also reshape her emotional connections – choosing new scents, new memories, and new emotions to create a sense of safety and belonging in her present life? The idea was both exciting and empowering.

walk through fear:
what do I need?

5 elements:

air - breathe
water - drink
earth - to provide + earth/grounding
fire - energy, inner fire, warmth
spirit - focus & spiritual connection
& LOVE

Back to the journal:

"Some of the most helpful sayings may seem like contradictions at first.
Don't let that throw you off.

Rather than resisting, try envisioning a different reality. There are countless parables about this in the Bible. Buddhists call it a **koan**—a paradox meant to deepen understanding.

Follow love. Wish the best for everyone involved. That includes **you**—because you are part of this, too. We are all connected.

A friend of mine had dyslexia. She was once advised not to hide behind it, not to define herself by it. If you reduce yourself to a single struggle, it's easy to slip into a victim mentality. But you are so much more than any challenge you face.

- Surrender to the here and now.

- Trust that there are good reasons for the present moment.
- Acknowledge why you may have disconnected from your emotions.
- Love and accept yourself unconditionally.
- Approach life holistically, and imagine that what you long for has **already** come true."

Take dyslexia, for example. Instead of focusing on limitations, shift your attention to your strengths:

- My communication skills are excellent.
- I have outstanding soft skills.
- I know how and where to find help and support.

And generally:

Where is my focus?
Am I dwelling on what I lack, or am I recognizing my **resources**?
Am I fixated on the problem, or am I exploring **solutions**?
Am I open to the possibility of **miracles**?

Why not?

And what does a miracle require? **A shift in perception.** A willingness to see things differently. A connection to the truth that we are more than our challenges.

Why not create that shift? Why not invite the miracle?

- take a deep breath
- did you drink enough?
- faith: is the glass half empty or half full?

That evening, Sarah wanted to go to bed early. But before she did, a sentence from her journal caught her attention:

'Change the image you have of yourself. Stop searching for the fulfillment of your desires only in the external world.'

Half-asleep, she took these words to heart. She closed her eyes and visualized herself as a successful author, fully embracing the idea. It was time to uncover her hidden talents.

CHAPTER 18 - OUT OF THE BLUE

Sarah focused on keeping a clear mind. The physical exercise was doing her good—she slept better at night and woke up feeling refreshed and energized. It wasn't just the packing—walking up and down the stairs slowly built her strength, boosted her fitness, and increased her endurance. The fresh air revitalized her from head to toe!

Spending more time outside, tidying up and letting go of things, felt unexpectedly liberating. Decluttering wasn't just a chore—it was fun!

Just one more sleep, and then the big day would finally be here. Tomorrow marked the start of something new, and nothing and no one was going to throw her off balance. She had learned so much, and now her thoughts were crystal clear.

Tomorrow was her fresh start—a new beginning for a new life.

Excitement bubbled up inside her. She could hardly wait!

Who was she kidding? Barely ten minutes later, her ex-boyfriend Andrew stood in the open doorway of her flat. Their eyes locked, and just like that, she had nowhere to run. A tremor rippled through her core, and her heart skipped a beat.

Breathe, she reminded herself.

Andrew stammered something, his words tangled in hesitation. It took her a moment to register that he was trying to apologize. But he wasn't done yet.

Another ten minutes passed, and in that time, he poured out everything – his regrets, his longing, his hopes. Then, in a voice that wavered just enough to reveal his vulnerability, he made her an offer that left her breathless.

A flicker of something familiar – something dangerous – shone in his eyes, and it threw her off balance.

Attempting to meet her gaze, he pleaded with her to give their relationship another chance.

'Sarah, my heart is on the line,' he pleaded. 'Please don't—'

Her pulse roared in her ears. Her knees felt unsteady, her chest tight with the weight of emotions she had tried so hard to bury.

She looked into the eyes she had loved so deeply. Maybe still did.

Sarah lost herself in his deep blue eyes for what felt like a short eternity. A rush of emotion hit her heart, but she couldn't tell if it was good or bad. 'Andrew,' Sarah gasped, struggling for air as she pushed him gently away. 'Give me some time to think. What's happening with you and Anna?'

'It didn't work. It was never meant to be,' Andrew replied quickly. 'It was just a brief fling, nothing substantial. Nothing real. It ended as fast as it started. I thought you already knew... we've been separated for a long time.'

Sarah had suspected as much. She never truly believed it was anything serious between them. Needing space, she walked into the kitchen, shut the door behind her, and stood there for a moment. She slowly poured herself a large glass of water, watching the liquid swirl in the glass. The sight of its clarity helped bring a brief sense of calm.

In that moment, Sarah realized the peace that could be found in the stillness of the storm. Giving herself the space to reflect, she took a deep, steadying breath.

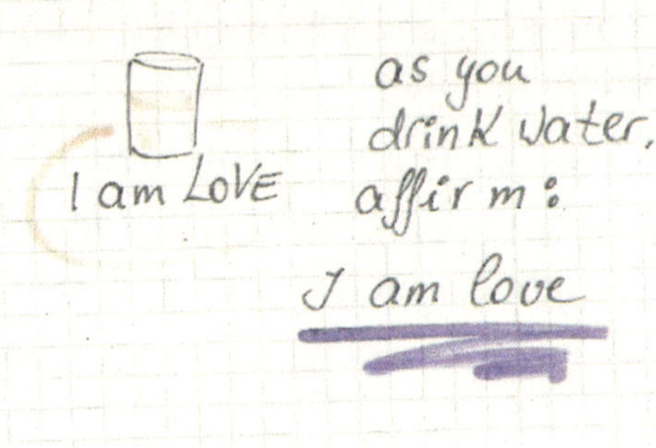

It was kind of sweet the way he pressed her, showing her how important she was to him. Finally, it seemed to dawn on him that she was the only one who held the key to his heart. Fair enough, Sarah thought, *though it only took him ages*—her thoughts laced with sarcasm.

For a brief moment, she felt satisfied with the outcome, but soon doubt crept in. 'Does this feel right?' she wondered. 'Is it real? Or is it just my ego, triumphing loudly and basking in the flattery?'

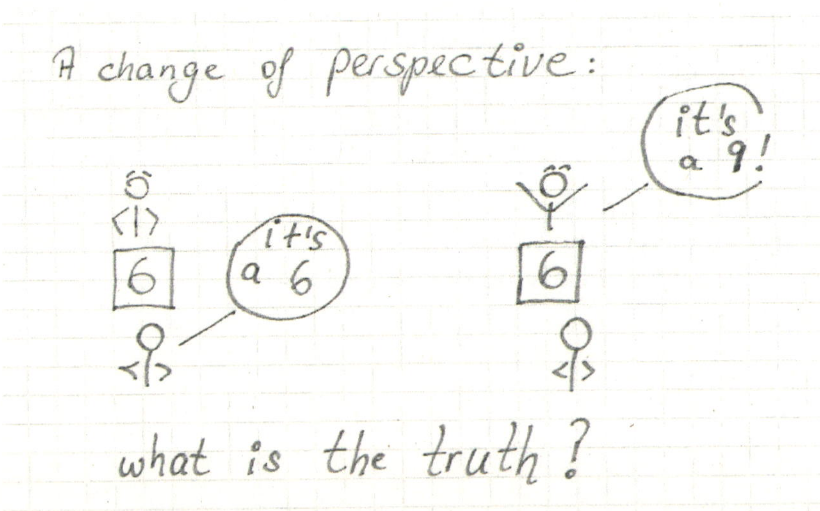

Whatever her decision would be, she knew she needed time. Time to reflect, to understand her true feelings, and to decide what was best for her heart.

Let your love be greater than your fear

Sarah exhaled deeply, the vital words from the journal echoing in her mind: '*I forgive you. And I forgive myself. And I will hand it over to the universe to sort it out!*' In a moment of soul-deep clarity, she stamped one foot on the floor. 'That's a command to my subconscious!' she declared firmly. She didn't want him to owe her anything. She didn't want to harbor hatred—because in the end, that would only poison her. Hatred wasn't good for the heart. She'd realized that weeks ago. And after all—the sparks were still flying between them.

With this realization, she summoned every ounce of courage she had to truly forgive him. Yes, it took courage! Because the ego feared making the wrong decision, of letting go too soon, of being vulnerable once again.

'Sarah!' Andrew's voice echoed softly through the door, full of pleading. 'If we're facing the naked truth, you have to be honest with yourself too. Lately, you've sent me to the doghouse more than once for no reason. It takes two to tango. Both of us made mistakes.

'And I still have deep feelings for you!' Andrew pleaded. 'Remember what you always said: love conquers all! Please, let us return to the round table.'

For a brief moment, time stood still. Sarah repeated the words out loud, almost as if to remind herself: 'I forgive you. And I mean it. And I forgive myself. I've made mistakes too. Even before you left me. Our relationship had already begun to fall apart long before this. You're right. But I don't want to use you as a scapegoat. I've made mistakes too. And I don't need any more trouble in my life. Let's forget about the past. It's time to bury the hatchet.'

Her words gave a sense of relief. After a brief pause, she continued, 'And I forgive Anna. We are all human, and nobody is perfect. Not even Anna.'

She listened to the silence that followed. Was that Andrew's breath? Or was he sobbing?

'I only wish the best for everyone involved,' Sarah added. 'But I need time and space right now. Space for myself... to rediscover myself.'

Andrew's response came in a flood of oaths, assurances, and promises, but Sarah remained resolute.

In the nick of time, he realized that it was no longer just about one misstep—it was much deeper than that. He saw, that Sarah had forgiven him with all her heart. And in that moment, he understood that he didn't want to love a version of her that he had created in his mind—a copy of his own ideal. He wanted to love the Sarah who was free, independent, and true to herself.

To do that, he knew he had to set her free.

It was time for a fresh start.

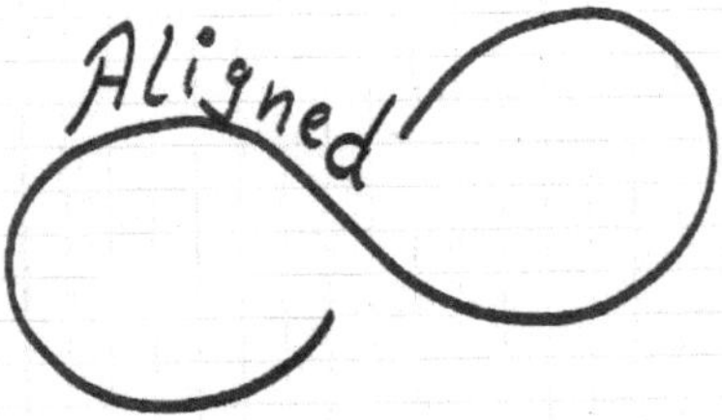

A deep bond
with
the
universal
source

CHAPTER 19 - CLARITY AT LAST

After what felt like endless hours, Andrew finally said goodbye, his heart heavy yet unburdened. He had spoken his truth.

Sarah, too, was left feeling a mix of emotions—bewildered, yet deeply relieved. She had found the right words. She had expressed herself with clarity and strength. More than anything, she was in awe of the quiet but unwavering guidance that had emerged from within.

The moment she decided to surrender her worries to the healing power of the universe, a deep sense of confidence filled her. Strength, not from force but from trust, surged through her. Perhaps it was her intuition. Perhaps it was her guardian angels. But in the end, she realized—it didn't matter whether they existed or not. What mattered was the feeling.

The feeling of being supported. The feeling of being loved. The deep knowing that if she asked for help, something greater than herself would respond. A presence, an energy—not bound to this world, but moving through it—lifting her higher, beyond fear, beyond doubt.

For the first time in a long time, Sarah felt truly at peace. She had faith in the future, even in its uncertainty. Whether her journey with Andrew was meant to continue or not—well, that would reveal itself in time. Right now, she was exactly where she needed to be.

Because in the end, there was only one certainty in life.

Love.

And love would always find a way to express itself.

Sarah realized she had been suppressing her anger for far too long. Deep down, she knew that wasn't healthy. *Don't let anger eat you up,* she reminded herself. Finally, she stood by her own truth. And instead of resisting something, she shifted her focus—choosing to stand *for* something instead. The subconscious seemed to respond better to that. **Energy flows where attention goes.**

Rather than being consumed by frustration over Andrew's behavior, she examined it more closely. What exactly had angered her? It was the way he had overstepped boundaries—making decisions that should have been hers alone. Choices that affected *her* life, *her* work. She was also frustrated with herself for giving in.

But instead of holding onto resentment, she turned it around. *From now on, I resolve to act with confidence. I embrace my right to make my own decisions, and I will stand by them!* She spoke the words aloud, feeling their power take root within her.

Then she recalled the supposed quote from Einstein: **"The most important question you can ask yourself is: Is the Universe a friendly place?"**

This time, Sarah's answer was a resounding *yes!* Oh, yes, it was!

It wasn't just a thought—it was a feeling that radiated through her entire body, resonating deep within her being.

'It truly is the most important question you can ask yourself,' she thought. At that moment, she fully grasped the weight of this question—and the profound consequences of her answer.

The way you answer this question internally shapes the energy and vibration you send out. *You reap what you sow.* If you believe the Universe is a friendly place, you align with that belief—resonating with its kindness, attracting it like a magnet. And if you don't? You may find only what reinforces your doubts.

Faith can move mountains. **To bring what you desire into your life, you must first *become* a vibrational match for it.**

This realization reminded Sarah to give herself what she longed for most: *love, affection, and recognition.*

What you nurture within will eventually be reflected in the world around you.

What is my new direction?

If Sarah believed the world was full of misery, she could manifest that reality. And if she saw the world as a beautiful place, she could bring more of that beauty into her life—step by step, moment by moment. *Inner peace could never be taken away by anyone.*

A wave of liberation washed over her, from head to toe. She felt free—free from the internal chains of old beliefs that no longer served her. And strangely, thanks to Andrew, she now carried an unshakable confidence that life would no longer surprise her in ways she couldn't handle. She was deeply rooted in herself, aligned with a new vibration.

She *felt* it.

As a result, body, mind, and soul were in perfect harmony. *This* was what holistic truly meant: a deep, unbreakable connection between all aspects of her being.

She took a sip of water, feeling its coolness spread through her mouth, grounding her in the present. She had arrived—*fully*—in the here and now. Calm. Clear. *Awake.*

This moment was her road to Damascus. Like a butterfly shedding its cocoon, she had outgrown her old self and emerged transformed.

Nikola Tesla once said: "**If you want to find the secrets of the universe, think in terms of energy, frequency, and vibration.**"

Sarah finally understood. ***Feelings*** **were the key.**

Was she acting out of fear?

Or was she choosing to act out of love?

She was surprised to realize that she was no longer annoyed with Andrew. The frustration that had once consumed her had simply dissolved.

Now, at last, she understood the passage in her journal about letting go of the victim mentality:

"You shed the victim mentality when you stop holding onto anger.
If something still makes you angry after a few days, it's worth looking deeper.
What exactly is resonating within you? What part of the situation is calling for your attention?"

I am ...

... homeowner

... successful

... happy

... overflowing with healing power

... and so on

Resonance is a musical term – when one string vibrates, another nearby can begin to resonate. The same applies to life experiences. **Why do we resonate with certain situations?**

When something or someone irritates us, it often reflects something within ourselves. **Perhaps a particular characteristic in another person triggers us because we either lack it or possess it in excess**. If we allow frustration to linger, it can quickly shift into a pessimistic mindset.

Is this already the beginning of a victim mentality? And if so, can we recognize it early enough to shift our perspective before it takes root?

Instead of simply reacting, we can ask:

- What exactly bothers me about this situation?
- What trait in the other person is triggering me?
- Is this something I need to develop or balance within myself?

<u>By looking inward, we move from irritation to insight – turning frustration into an opportunity for growth.</u>

There is always a reason we are drawn to certain experiences—they serve as mirrors, reflecting what our soul seeks to balance. **Deep down, we all strive for equilibrium, a state of harmony within ourselves.**

This is where classic **shadow work** comes in.

The "shadow" represents the parts of ourselves we suppress—the traits we don't want to acknowledge or show the world. These may be aspects of our character that society discourages or qualities we fear embracing. But once we recognize them, we can begin to integrate and heal them.

Perhaps we lack a certain trait and subconsciously resent those who embody it. Or maybe we have too much of it, and it overwhelms us. Either way, awareness is the first step to resolution.

Reading these lines, Sarah reflected on how much Andrew's behavior used to trigger her—his habit of making decisions without considering her input. Now, she saw it differently. It had frustrated her because, at the time, she lacked self-determination. His actions had shone a light on the very thing she needed to develop within herself.

Perhaps negative emotions aren't obstacles but signposts. They highlight the imbalances we need to address. The Universe isn't punishing us—it's guiding us toward growth.

don't forget: a healthy balance

That night, Sarah went to bed with a completely different feeling – one of deep inner peace. Pure bliss.

It felt as though she had finally accepted her struggles rather than resisting them. *And isn't that one of life's greatest tasks?* she mused. *To accept and transform our fate, to forgive our parents for their mistakes, and, in time, to forgive ourselves?* True surrender. True letting go.

She made a decision – mind, body, and soul deserved to be in harmony. *Why not treat myself to something truly restorative?* A holistic treatment sounded perfect. A massage to release lingering stress, a jog to shake off old energy, or maybe even dancing – losing herself in the rhythm of pure joy.

She smiled as she thought of the affirmations she wanted to anchor deep within:
'I love myself exactly as I am.'
'I embrace everything that serves my higher self and supports my well-being.'

Sarah remembered that the power of imagination worked best in those in-between moments – just before falling asleep or right after waking up.

Closing her eyes, she visualized herself in her new flat, safe and happy, her heart overflowing with joy. A wave of warmth spread through her, wrapping her in comfort as she drifted off to sleep.

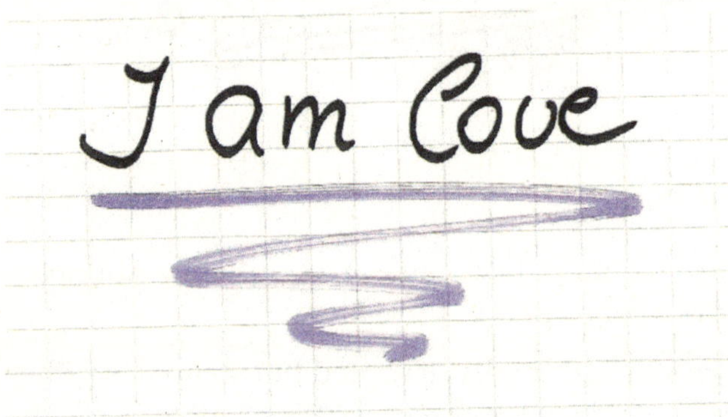

CHAPTER 20 - FINALLY AT HOME

The next day, everything unfolded just as Sarah had imagined. Her friends helped her carry boxes, shifting everything into her new home. And just as she had finally given her soul a home within her body, she now gave her body a home in her new flat. It felt more than great—it felt right.

One of her friends paused mid-box lift and studied her. 'Wow, Sarah, you look so different! You *glow*. What have you been doing? Was it that journal you told me about?'

Sarah smiled. 'Oh, you know,' she said lightly, 'it wasn't just about reading the journal; it was about putting the advice into practice and truly integrating it into my life. Really understanding what those insights had to do with my own life. That was the key. We all have these great sayings printed on our teacups, but if you go deeper, you can start rewriting the old patterns that don't serve you anymore.'

She set down a box and continued, 'I made a list, looked at where I needed to take responsibility again. In the past, I'd read these things but never really followed through. Then I thought, *if this works for small things, why not try it on the big things?* And you know what? I actually enjoyed the process!'

Her friend, now distracted by Sarah's cat, nodded thoughtfully. Sarah added, 'And here's the most important part—if something goes wrong, forgive yourself. No one is perfect. And who knows? Maybe whatever happened was meant to teach us something. When you look at the bigger picture, you realize… maybe we *needed* that experience to know what we don't want.

If you completely surrender to your destiny, you can find inner peace—even when everything else seems to be falling apart. True transformation happens in that state of surrender,' Sarah said.

'I wouldn't even know where to start...' her friend admitted, looking uncertain.

'I know what you mean,' replied Sarah. 'Yes, it takes courage. For me, the closer I faced my fears, the smaller they became. The good thing is, with many methods, you no longer have to go through the old negative experience. You don't have to feel that again. Why don't you go to a good alternative practitioner or counselor? That would certainly help you to get started.'

Sarah beamed at her old, dear friend and then added playfully, 'Or you could ask my grandma to adopt you!'

They laughed and hugged each other, feeling their deep connection.

In the evening, they gathered around the new yet familiar kitchen table, celebrating with a glass of wine and hearty 'spag-bol' that her aunt had delivered in large pots. Sarah was ravenous, her appetite mirroring her newfound zest for life – unparalleled and electrifying. Life felt perfect! She grinned from ear to ear, soaking in the warmth of the moment. The lively atmosphere in the kitchen transported her back to the best times in Italy, where the whole family would sit around the table, talking, laughing, and simply being happy. That same energy filled the room now—love, joy, and a deep passion for life pulsed through her.

And just like that, as they sat together, she realized this was exactly how she had envisioned it. So, manifesting did work after all! **But only, it seemed, when approached holistically. Feelings mattered.** When she truly felt content deep in her heart and imagined that her desires had already come to life, they somehow did. That was the secret her grandma had always spoken about—suddenly, it all made sense.

Where attention goes, energy flows. Feel the abundance, love, and connection to Source. Stay connected. Be that Source Energy Being you are meant to be!

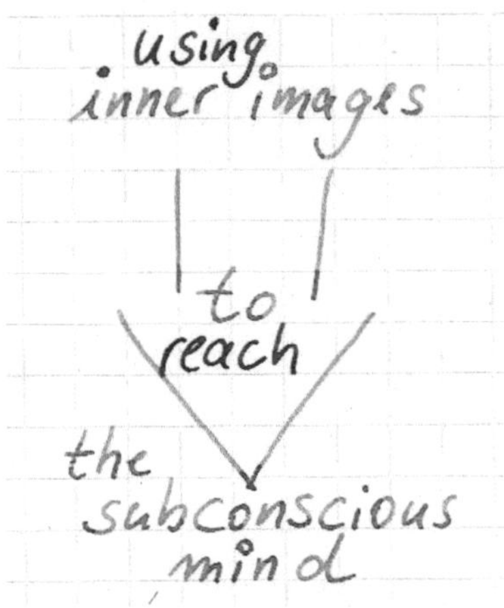

Sarah was still reflecting, her thoughts swirling with excitement. *Wow, if this works on a 'small' scale, why not on a 'big' scale too? Think big!* Perhaps next time, she'd manifest a villa instead. But then again—who would clean all those rooms? She chuckled at the thought. In reality, all she truly needed was space for herself and her cats. Right now, the park around the corner felt far more valuable than a grand estate.

Laughter, joy, and togetherness—those were the things that truly mattered. What role did material possessions play in any of it? None. Lighten up, Sarah, she reminded herself. It's not about where you are, but how you feel.

It's not about the physical items one manifests, but about the version of you that already has them—or the version of you that doesn't care about external circumstances.

'Hey,' Grandad giggled, 'the chutney is still good, it's only eleven years old. The lid's still unopened. Who has the courage to try it?' His laughter was infectious. It was an inside joke—Grandma and Grandad never threw anything away, especially not homemade chutney.

'Wow, I'm living on the edge! I'll have a go!' Dad laughed.

'Don't forget to give the empty jar back to Grandma! Otherwise, you'll have lived on the edge, and it's over pretty quick!' Grandad replied.

Everyone burst into laughter. Not returning empty jars was considered a capital sin in their family.

Grandma yelped, 'My old diary, my journal! I haven't seen this for a long time!' She took the old journal from the shelf into her hands.

'Yes, Grandma. A lifesaver! Thank you so much for this!' Sarah said with a grateful smile. 'I was looking high and low for answers. I didn't realize that help could be closer than we think.'

Looking back, that time of crisis had turned out to be the best thing that could have happened to Sarah. It had helped her find her way back to herself.

There was still a way to go, but deep down, she knew she had a reliable compass in her hands. This compass was like a lamp, lighting the way when it was dark and hollow around her—a compass to navigate her to inner peace.

Her soul felt elated and spirited. Inwardly, a picture of happiness emerged. Colourful flowers bloomed from the once barren desert ground, reflecting her renewed love of life. Her heart leapt with joy, and a warm, happy feeling ran up her spine.

It lasted only a brief moment, but she resolved to be more aware of such beautiful sensations from now on.

She was ready to embrace loving vibrations and high energies.

She already felt at home in her new flat. Somehow, she couldn't wait to see what life had in store for her. Big adventures awaited her, and deep down, she knew it.

She was filled with anticipation and love.

Sources of Inspiration:

I was accompanied and inspired on my path by:

Irenka Herbert, thank you for reminding me of my inner strength over 20 years ago (RIP)

Marianne Bresgen, shamanartwork, Heimbach

Maya de Vries, EFT- and TBT-trainer (Trauma Buster Technique), Cologne

Jürgen Lehmacher, Bewusst besser Leben, Gemünd

Power questions: freely adapted from Noah St. John

Visualisation technique loosely based on Neville Goddard: 'Self talk creates reality'

Thanks to Werner Hoffmann. You gave me the right hint at the right moment

And many more... ∞ Thank you

Glossar:

Holistic p. 7 - body, mind, soul and spiritual connection to the unmanifested (God)

Melancholic p. 15 – a range of emotions when suffering from world-weariness and gloom

Visualising p. 15 – to visualise something

Intuition p. 16 – an inner inspiration, inner voice... divine inspiration...

Manifest p. 16 – achieve a desired state, not only mentally but also in reality

Spiritual p. 19 - Spirituality is often used to describe the spiritual connection to a higher entity. A spiritual experience is, for example, when we feel connected to a higher authority within ourselves and feel fulfilled as a result

Eureka p. 22 - An exclamation indicating sudden discovery

Mantra p. 28 – Mantras are sacred words that are chanted or recited aloud or in thought. Some are thousands of years old and are used as a tool for quieting the mind

Ritual p. 31 – A sacred ceremony or a mystical act that brings the participants closer to the divine. Repetitions that are an integral part of a daily or annual rhythm. Nowadays there are also rituals that have no spiritual significance. For example, blowing out candles on a birthday cake

primordial source (or the unmanifested) p. 47 – original source of our being/ God

tapping acupressure p. 69 – Light tapping on certain acupressure or meridian points is intended to rebalance the energy system. No needles are used as in acupuncture

Trauma p. 71 – is a strong emotional and/or physical shock, with or without acute pain, which can last for a long time. It is usually triggered by a bad experience, an accident or an attack

Resource p. 75 - A resource is a means of achieving something. Food, for example, is a resource. We speak of intangible resources when we talk about inner strength or resilience, for example

koan p. 124 – a seemingly paradoxical statement used as a tool to push past the limitations of a conceptual mind

Homeostasis p. 156 – Striving for a balance through self-regulation (example page 71: nature seeks balance)

Contents:

Defining trust. What do I trust in?

Current Core Values. Which values are important to me now?

Sources of Inspiration. What inspires me?

Seeking External Help vs. Self-Empowerment. Wait for help from outside or take matters into your own hands from within?

Living a Self-Determined Life

Mirror Work (What Annoys Me About Others?)

Be yourself: a source of energy

Redefining Your Own Values

Bypassing the Critical Mind to Access the Subconscious

Transforming Inherited Blockages and Emotional Heritage

Restructuring Old Belief Patterns

Improving Relationships

Preventing Burnout

Redirecting Life's Path. Giving life a new direction

Personal Development and Individual Fulfillment

Inner Peace - Emotional Stability

Shame and guilt

Secondary Gains from Illness

Counting Your Blessings

Homeostasis: Natural Balance

Sarah's mantra: I thank the universe for this wonderful opportunity ... (put in what you wish for. 21 days say and feel it in the morning shortly after waking up and in the evening shortly before going to sleep. Feel it in your whole body...)

About the author:

Myriam Adams (born 1971) grew up with her grandparents in the Eifel region. Since she can remember, her favourite place was the forest. She later moved in with her parents in Düsseldorf and worked in administration after completing her apprenticeship. From 1995 to 2007, Myriam Adams lived in Wales, where her interest in alternative self-help methods was awakened. In 2006, she set up her own business as a holistic massage therapist (Holistic Massage Therapist, ITEC, UK) and coach.

Myriam Adams offers seminars and workshops on the topics of 'Holistic Self-Discovery' and 'Working with the Subconscious'.

The current focus of her work as a soul archaeologist is 'Resolving the transgenerational transmission of emotional stress' and 'Successfully transforming victim mentality'.

Further information and current dates can be found on her websites:

www.sarahscompass.net

www.holistic-eft.com

Photo: Julian Hoffmeister

* 9 7 8 3 9 8 2 7 2 0 5 0 0 *
BV - #0051 - 150425 - C0 - 210/148/9 - PB - 9783982720500 - Matt Lamination